# A CONTROVERSIAL CLERGYMAN

Provocative Newspaper Articles to Foster Critical Thinking on Social, Societal, Legal, Church and Public Speaking Matters

### CLINTON CHISHOLM

Extra MILE Innovators
Kingston, Jamaica W.I.

**Copyright © 2019 by Clinton A. Chisholm**

ISBN-13: 978-1-62676-653-2

ALL RIGHTS RESERVED

Without limiting the rights under copyright reserved above, no part of this publication may be reproduced, stored in or introduced into a retrieval system, or transmitted, in any form, or by any means (electronic, mechanical, photocopying, recording, or otherwise), without the prior contractual or written permission of the copyright owner of this work.

· · · · · ·

Published by
Extra MILE Innovators
21 Phoenix Avenue,
Kingston 10, Jamaica W.I.
www.extramileja.com
administrator@extramileja.com
Tele: (1876) 782-9893

Cover Designed by Phil Lashley
lashleyupload@gmail.com

Author Contact

For consultation, feedback or speaking engagements contact the author at cchisholm81@gmail.com

# ENDORSEMENTS

In columns marked by cogent argumentation communicated in lucid prose, Clinton Chisholm shares reflections on a wide range of issues of concern to his target audience. The insights he shares are informed and illuminating. The columns may serve as splendid conversation starters that can help readers and discussion groups unearth perspectives they previously failed to consider.

>Rev. Dr. Neville Callam
>Baptist World Alliance General Secretary Emeritus

. . . . . . .

I would encourage educators to consider including [Chisholm's] text on the list of required reading for the older students. I believe that this would prove to be most beneficial as we seek to enable them to develop and hone that important 21st century skill of Critical Thinking which appears to be disappearing from among even those considered to be the most erudite in our society.

>Sharon Reid (Mrs.)
>Principal, St. Andrew High School for Girls

. . . . . . .

This book comprises a collection of articles that was previously written for two Jamaican newspapers. Chisholm's discourse type is argumentation, presented in a manner that is unique in its simultaneous seriousness and seemingly provocative flippancy. Chisholm addresses a wide range of themes and subjects such as legal matters, church matters and social matters, as well as numerous current events and affairs.

Well-written and carefully structured, the articles sometimes advance bold, unconventional claims through the effective employment of fitting rhetorical modes and stylistic features. The language and style are riveting and will cause the reader to laugh with hilarity, but also to stop, think and interrogate the seriousness underlying the humour.

Chisholm is a skillful writer who employs sarcasm, irony, overstatement, understatement supported by a wide range of organizing principles as a means of pulling readers into his texts. The reader in turn, is forced to draw on several reading strategies in order to read at different levels and interpret, synthesize and construct meaning from the texts.

Several articles are propelled by controversy which is often intriguing, but the writer's examples, explanations, evidence and obvious knowledge of his topics help to establish credibility. Each article is followed by discussion questions designed to encourage readers to assess the logic of his arguments, judge his credibility and test his knowledge of the subjects he debates.

This book will serve as a very interesting way of teaching students to read actively and think critically and analytically. Chisholm's ability to bring new dimensions to the debate around each topic is decidedly important in forcing readers to read between the lines and underneath the many layers of meanings of words and sentences.

Paulette A. Ramsay
Professor of Afro-Hispanic Studies,
The University of the West Indies, Mona Campus

# DEDICATION

To my Chisholm clan: wife, Flora Vivienne; children, Antoinette Vivienne (Lashley), Samuel Jacques and grandson Cameron Clinton for whom I'll readily give my life and reluctantly take a life.

# INTRODUCTION

In this collection those who were, up to now, unaware of the mischievous nature of my mind and the frank even blunt style of my written and oral presentations, will find evidence beyond reasonable doubt.

In light of this confession I can do no better than presumptuously borrow a prayer from Samuel Johnson (that 18th century English intellectual) who, in the 2nd volume of his Dictionary wrote:

"O God, Who hast hitherto supported me, enable me to proceed in this labour, and in the whole task of my present state; that when I shall render up at the last day an account of the talent committed to me, I may receive pardon for the sake of Jesus Christ." (Cited in John W. Montgomery, Christ as Centre and Circumference: Essays Theological, Cultural and Polemic, 2012, 546)

As the subtitle says, the book is intended to foster critical thinking by providing newspaper examples under five sections (social issues, societal concerns, legal affairs, Church matters and miscellaneous) with questions at the end of each article for individual reflection or group discussion.

The discussion could be part of a secondary or tertiary-level English language or literature class dealing with comprehension or literary intent/devices or for communication studies in a Community College class or for ethical discussion/debate in a Religious education class or a Youth Fellowship/Sabbath or Sunday School class. Explore for instance, the pieces on Abortion or on the buggery law, sex scandal and the Church, or on values within the social issues and societal concerns sections.

Students of law and their lecturers will derive intellectual food reading about the views of the renowned Natural Law legal philosopher John Finnis, on homosexuality and by examining my logical analysis of the celebrated Caleb Orozco ruling from the Chief Justice of Belize plus my logical chiding of a suggestion from Jamaica's current Minister of Justice (2019).

Though the exercise will be uncomfortable for most, while examining the Church matters section, Church leaders should find valuable nuggets from my appeal for critical thinking in church from pulpit and pew alike and are invited to engender discussion about my informed but mischievous thoughts on the Church and culture as well as dealing with the sore and sensitive matter of clergy sexual abuse.

The final section of the book, miscellaneous, provides little known pointers on mastering pronunciation that should prove very helpful to Ministers of government, lecturers, business executives, Preachers and all others involved in public speaking.

I do not ask you, dear Reader, to agree with my ideas, but simply ask that you honestly engage your critical mind with mine and dare to follow where the evidence and argumentation may lead you.

So come, let us reason together!

# TABLE OF CONTENTS

PART 1: SOCIAL ISSUES .......................................... 1

Article 1: Unchangeable Behaviour: A Challenge for Psychiatry? ................................................. 2

Article 2: Hope: Fundamental but Fragile ........ 5

Article 3: The Petrojam Saga: A Neglected Factor ...................................................................... 10

Article 4: Beyond Immorality ........................... 16

Article 5: Defending and Dismantling the Buggery Law Sloppily ...................................... 21

Article 6: Archbishop John Holder on Sodom/Gomorrah and Modern Sodomy Laws ...................................................................... 26

Article 7: Legal Philosopher John Finnis on Homosexuality ................................................. 32

Part II: SOCIETAL CONCERNS ........................... 37

Article 8: What's so Wrong With…If? .............. 38

Article 9: Playing Deadly Games with Tobacco… ...................................................................... 44

Article 10: Unpalatable Food for Thought ........ 47

Article 11: How Religion Poisons Everything … 50

Article 12: Ethical Leadership: Definition and Defense ............................................................ 56

Article 13: The Knowledge vs. Belief Confusion ............................................................................63

Article 14: An Abortion Primer ........................ 67

Article 15: Of Illegal Drugs, Guns and Sex ........ 73

Article 16: The 'Own Body Argument': Sense and Nonsense ........................................................ 77

Article 17: Pro-Choicers and the 'Not a Person' Argument ....................................................... 82

Article 18: The Bible and Indictable Ignorance 87

## PART III: LEGAL AFFAIRS ................................ 92

Article 19: Judicial Courage: Ruling vs. Reasoning ................................................................... 93

Article 20: Law and Ethics: Natural or Unnatural Bedfellows? .................................................. 101

Article 21: Michael, be Fair to God ................ 107

Article 22: Chuck Challenging Church's Old Teachings ..................................................... 113

## PART IV: CHURCH MATTERS .......................... 116

Article 23: Understanding and Dealing with Clergy Sexual Abuse .................................... 117

Article 24: Critical Thinking and the Church .130

Article 25: The Church and Culture ............... 135

Article 26: Compromised Democracy in Church and State Elections? ........................................ 141

Part V: PUBLIC SPEAKING AND MISCELLANEOUS ....................................... 144

Article 27: Christopher Hitchens: An Intellectual Post-Mortem? ............................................... 145

Article 28: The Yellow Pages Storm in a Thimble.. .................................................................. 150

Article 29: Stimulus and Response, Revisited ................................................................ ....153

Article 30: Slavery in the Bible: Michael Abrahams's Reading Problems .................... 157

Article 31: The Presumption of Resolutions ... 164

Article 32: For Public Speakers and Singers .. 168

Article 33: Public Speaking: Problems and Solutions ....................................................... 172

CONCLUSION ................................................. 176

ACKNOWLEDGEMENTS ............................ 178

REFERENCES ................................................ 179

ABOUT THE AUTHOR ................................ 183

# Part I

# SOCIAL ISSUES

# Article 1

## UNCHANGEABLE BEHAVIOUR: A CHALLENGE FOR PSYCHIATRY?

**Gist**: The logic of the legal ban on psychological attempts at behaviour change for homosexuals is explored

It is said that fools rush in where angels fear to tread, so pardon my folly. In fact it may be worse, I may be about to take my life into my own hands, but then I believe in resurrection.

Reparative therapy (behavior change) for homosexuals is seen by many therapists, gay and straight alike, as 'clinical crap' (my obnoxious words, not theirs) because it not only does not work but, for many if not most or all, it cannot work. The confessions and apologies of Alan Chambers, former head of the now-closed Exodus International (a ministry for persons with unwanted same-sex attractions and activity) seem to corroborate this view. But this raises some awkward questions for Psychiatry and related disciplines.

What is it about homosexuality that makes it so resistant to psychotherapy and clinical behavior modification interventions? I gather from friends in the field of Psychology that behaviors that are usually associated with personality disorders are often difficult to treat and so are behaviors resulting from bipolar disorder and schizophrenia. Psychiatrists should do us the favour of explaining why it is clinically pointless to attempt behavior change even in a person who does not want to continue in a same-sex liaison.

Is it because this relates to **sexual intercourse**? Might it also then be clinically pointless to attempt behavior change in any person who desires to give up fornication, adultery, bestiality, incest or any other sexual attraction and practice? We need to know, help us please.

What then is the future of the now popular reparative justice programmes where behavior change is emphasized over and even replaces imprisonment? Money well-spent or wasted on a futile venture? Just asking.

## SOCIAL ISSUES

Then, since I have already put my life in my hand, indulge me a bit further. Neurosurgeons treat brain-related maladies. What exactly do Psychiatrists and Psychologists treat within humans since the *psyche* (whether soul, self or mind) is immaterial and invisible? Just asking, especially of those who are hard-nosed materialists and/or atheists.

Is my problem too much time as an unemployed person or have I fallen in love with a coffin?

Jamaica Gleaner, Observer 27/7/13

# DISCUSSION QUESTIONS

1. In what specific way has the article nudged you to think deeper on its subject matter?

2. What literary device(s) does the writer use in the article and how successful was the effort?

3. Comment on the strongest and the weakest argument advanced in the article.

# Article 2

## HOPE: FUNDAMENTAL BUT FRAGILE

**Gist**: Advice on hope for all, especially leadership rivals in the PNP

Whether it is Peter Bunting or Peter Phillips re the leadership of their political party, or anyone of us in our daily lives, all humans are creatures of hope.

But what really is hope? In a nutshell, hope is confident assurance about the 'not yet.' Be that 'not yet' near (later today) or far (September or when the road repairs are done), we are all enmeshed in some degree of confident assurance about it. Be it about something simple or trite (crossing a road, expecting a salary cheque or bank upload of salary), significant and life-changing (surgery, promised promotion), none of us can truly avoid indulging hope in our lives.

Indeed, even the person who is planning to or commits suicide to put an end to his/her problems is indulging hope. He or she hopes death will end it all, but what if there is an afterlife with rewards and punishments as some religionists claim?

Hope is fundamental in life, but oh so fragile. Messrs. Bunting and Phillips in particular should recall the fragility of political hope.

This was vividly illustrated in Jamaican political life more than once but classically in my view in October 1980 when the PNP campaigned on the mantra "150 thousand strong can't be wrong," yet lost in a landslide defeat at the polls. Hope disappointed the PNP then as much as hope disappointed the JLP in December 2011.

Hope, necessary and fundamental, but oh so fragile a commodity in life.

On February 11, 2011 the news broke that President Hosni Mubarak of Egypt had resigned, one day after he shocked protestors in Egypt by saying he would not step down from power and 'would not be separated from Egyptian soil until his body was

## A CONTROVERSIAL CLERGYMAN

below the soil'. On what was his hope of remaining in power resting the day before, i.e. February 10?

Whether you are religious, irreligious, a skeptic, an atheist, an agnostic, or whatever, you are a creature of hope – a person who entertains confident assurance about a 'not yet.'

What hope promises provides pleasure, but that hope might not deliver the goods promised produces an element of pain.

It is the guarantee or the guarantor that grounds your hope which determines whether your hope is just 'blind optimism' or 'confident realism.'

While studying in England (1990-92) two interviews of national importance caught my attention. The one interview was with David Frost, sharp TV host, and a Mr. Morley, Alexander Morley, I think, one of the moving forces behind the Channel Tunnel, the proposed undersea rail tunnel linking Britain and France. The other interview involved Mrs. Margaret Thatcher, then Prime Minister.

The Thatcher interview was occasioned by rumours that Mrs. Thatcher was contemplating resignation as P.M. In response, Mrs. Thatcher said words to the effect, "I shall be around as P.M. for a long time." In less than a week, she had resigned. Hope, built on the fragile support of her colleagues in Parliament, had disappointed her and for all I

## SOCIAL ISSUES

know up to her death she was still smarting from the pain of frustrated political hope.

In the other British incident David Frost was interviewing Alexander Morley in 1990 I think, and wanted an indication of the opening date for the Channel Tunnel. Mr. Morley very guardedly indicated that they were hoping for a 1993 start. Frost pressed for a more definite date and chided the element of hope in Morley's reply, to which Morley wisely replied, "We can only hope that by 1993 it will be functional, but we can't be sure. Are you sure you'll be around in 1993?"

There is a folk tradition in Jamaica, maybe borrowed from elsewhere, which instructs that, when you are alone in a dark area and afraid, you should whistle or hum a song to keep your company. Not a sensible suggestion at all because you are still the only one there and attracting attention by the sound you are making.

I am mischievously eager to see how Mr. Bunting's leadership challenge works out, but I urge him, Dr. Phillips and all of us, to give more serious thought to the double edge of hope. It is fundamental and fragile.

Jamaica Observer 1/7/19

A CONTROVERSIAL CLERGYMAN

# DISCUSSION QUESTIONS

1. What in the article, if anything, prompted you to give more serious thought to its central theme?

2. In your view would Messrs. Bunting or Phillips take the article with any degree of seriousness? Why or why not?

3. Was the author's literary intent achieved and on what is your answer based?

# Article 3

## THE PETROJAM SAGA: A NEGLECTED FACTOR

**Gist**: An ethical analysis of the saga

I would hazard a guess that it is a very rare person, however professedly sanctified, who has not, in mind at least, come close to using expletives in describing the sordid saga that has been unfolding about sections of the higher echelons of Petrojam.

For me, and I am not known to mince words even from a pulpit, it is an unbridled damnable disgrace (pardon my Ugaritic or check an Oxford dictionary for the meanings of damnable). Maybe I just need Jesus!

# A CONTROVERSIAL CLERGYMAN

I have listened to and read the evidence of people's outrage at what has been allowed to happen at the Petroleum Corporation of Jamaica (PCJ) contrary to law, best business practices and plain common sense for so many years.

The primary neglected factor for me though is the implied and as yet unexplored justification of our disgust and outrage. Don't seek to collect a tin of condensed milk by hunting me down and turning me into Bellevue. Hear me out a bit.

Ok, so laws [may] have been broken, best practices disregarded, etc., etc., so what, Critic, if the ethical principle you espouse and defend normally is relativism? By relativism I mean simply the view that nothing is always right or wrong in essence, but every act, intention, motive depends on situation or circumstance for an evaluative decision.

I readily plead guilty to the charge of being 'weird' [philosophically]. Do our legal commentators on the saga realise that even laws have ethical underpinnings? Who in our law schools teach the ethics of jurisprudence? Just asking, calm down.

So. I ask again what's so wrong with what has been happening under both political regimes at PCJ if relativism rules? After all, do some of our societal intellectuals subscribe to a higher ethical principle than the rugged relativistic principle "man haffi eat a food?" Like seriously?

If nothing is always wrong then almost anything could be right, depending on... I have suggested mischievously in presentations to groups of Christian University/College students that they ask their lecturers, whom they know to be averse to absolutism, why they monitor every single exam to ensure that no one ever cheats. Why not allow students to cheat on the most important exam (just one) in their academic life in the student's reckoning, if cheating is not always wrong?

By absolutism I mean the view that some things (acts, intentions, motives), not all things, are always wrong or right in essence regardless of situation or circumstance.

At the risk of being unfriended by my lawyer friends, I maintain that there is nothing more absolutist in ethos than the legal oath/affirmation taken by witnesses. Ponder the oath "I swear by [some deity, not necessarily Almighty God, that binds your conscience to truth-telling, cf. R v Hinds I think] that the evidence I shall give to the court shall be the truth [no full stop] the whole truth [no full stop] and **nothing but the truth.**" No relativistic elbow room is allowed! Notice, as well, that adherence to this absolutist declaration is further tested by cross examination. Our Courts cannot operate on a lesser standard if justice is to be the end result.

For years now I have been trying, in my periodic submissions to our newspapers, to promote my special definition of integrity which is "whole-hearted abiding fidelity to wholesome abiding principles." Every word is carefully chosen and modification reduces its force and value. Let's test a few modifications.

Mod. 1 '[occasional] fidelity to wholesome, abiding principles.' Not helpful at all.

Mod. 2 'abiding fidelity to unwholesome abiding principles.' Detrimental!

Mod. 3 'abiding fidelity to [?] principles.' Dubious and dangerous!

Despite its veneer of practical and conceptual attractiveness, relativism is fatally flawed. There are seven fatal flaws of relativism identified by Francis Beckwith & Gregory Koukl, in their 1998 book, *Relativism: Feet Firmly Planted in Mid-air* ( 61-69).

1. *Relativists can't accuse others of wrongdoing.*

If there is no objective wrong or right then moral outrage at whatever (Hitler, Idi Amin, Saddam Hussein or 9/11) is no more than a personal opinion.

# SOCIAL ISSUES

*2. Relativists can't complain about the problem of evil re the existence of God.*

Without objective evil the argument fails. Concede objective evil and objective good, as a standard, is pulled in.

*3. Relativists can't defensibly place blame or accept praise.*

Without absolutes, nothing is ultimately praiseworthy or blameworthy. Relativists studiously avoid blame but swallow praise without comment, but on what logical basis?

*4. Relativists can't make charges of unfairness or injustice.*

Both concepts make sense only on the existence of objective standards of fairness and justice.

*5. Relativists can't improve their morality.*

If there is no better way, there can be no improvement or even the moral impulse to improve. Morals may change but not improve.

*6. Relativists can't hold meaningful moral discussions.*

Silence on moral issues would be the most consistent option for relativists. Even the minimalist statement 'you can't push your morality on me' is not allowed because it qualifies as a moral rule.

7. *Relativists can't even promote the obligation of tolerance.*

Tolerance, properly understood, is putting up with what you disagree with. But on what basis is there genuine disagreement if there are no objective standards of the right and the true?

We ought to register disgust and outrage at the Petrojam saga but with due regard for the neglected ethical factors I have raised here.

Jamaica Observer 20/12/18

## DISCUSSION QUESTIONS

1. What factual error or logical weakness can you identify in the article?

2. Why is the rampancy of corruption more a failure in law enforcement than a failure in human ability to do what's right?

3. How were you helped, if at all, in deepening your own analysis of the saga?

# Article 4

## BEYOND IMMORALITY

**Gist**: The Church and a Sex Scandal

The Church of Jesus Christ (all groupings including Moravians) should not register alarm or surprise at the mixed flock of birds that has swarmed around us and will continue so to do (most of the birds being john crows or dead flesh eaters but not all), because we have provided the dead flesh that such birds delight in tearing to bits.

I confess that owing to a barrage of work over the past few weeks I came to the sex scandal saga (soap opera, to be continued?) a bit late in the day, and registered bewilderment at bits and pieces of the allegations levelled at my clergy Brother Rupert

Clarke (yes, he is still my brother though I don't think I know him personally) that I heard or read and I responded with my usual "behold I show you a mystery" to things that baffle my mind.

Father Raulston Nembhard's *Observer* column on Wednesday (January 11, 2017) spoke for me and to me and I emailed him and said as much.

Concern for the young miss in the saga should be extended to her whole family regardless of what may eventually be proven in court.

The Church in general has been far too reluctant to talk about things sexual in the settings where most of our people show up (Saturday or Sunday morning worship services). Relegating such discussions to mid-week evening/night meetings where comparatively few attend is deliberately failing to scratch where people continue to itch.

It is my long-held belief, and I open my CD **Plain Talk on Sex** with it, that "if you have never felt a strong pull to sexual intercourse you are too young, too old or too lie!"

I go stronger now, whether you are a parson or not. As a Christian, if you claim that you have never struggled with a temptation to sexual immorality you are extremely rare or you need to be reminded of Rev. 21:8 "...all liars have their part in the lake of fire."

## SOCIAL ISSUES

I have suggested to congregations that, with reference to our confessional prayer life before God, we go beyond owning up to actual sin as S-I-N and acknowledge to God a personal proneness (leaning) to certain sins. Praying this way shows acute awareness of the weak areas in my personal life and reminds me that in these areas sin is not just merely possible or probable for all persons but likely for me personally. Thus, it humanizes me.

Praying this way does another delightful thing; it sensitizes me concerning other Christians who sin or do unlawful things. So, I avoid two extremes in response to such persons, the extreme of condemnation and of compromise. The recommended middle road is compassion.

Quite frankly, though hard to swallow as an idea, we all should ponder the thought that we may not have committed the sins of others not because we lack the desire for those sins or similar ones, but because we simply lacked the opportunity that others had or created. What if desire and opportunity came together in my life, would I not be 'john crow food' as others?

I was shot between my spiritual eyes years ago by a statement that I read from Christian philosopher Dallas Willard. He said:

> The thought of sin is not sin and is not even temptation. Temptation is the thought plus the inclination to sin – possibly manifested by lingering over the thought or seeking it out. But sin itself is when we inwardly say 'yes' to temptation, **when we would do the deed, even though we do not actually do it**. (*Renovation of the Heart*, p.33, my emphasis)

When we struggle unsuccessfully with some sexual temptation we may need, in addition to prayer/fasting, serious psychiatric help.

Struggling unsuccessfully with a proneness to sexual intercourse with minors, i.e. feeling a compulsion to have sexual intercourse with minors (paedophilia), I gather from my friends in Psychology, suggests a need for deep psychotherapy.

Some behaviours, in my weird mind though, go beyond immorality and illegality and border on lunacy!

Still, we all need to heed the wise caution of Attorney Bert Samuels who chided the media (formal and social) for seeming to forget that an accused person has legal rights too until the case is disposed of in court. What we unlearned folk and even lawyers call an 'open and shut case' by the

SOCIAL ISSUES

appearance of the allegations are at times not that at all!

-Jamaica Observer 17/1/17

## **DISCUSSION QUESTIONS**

1. In what way is this a wake-up call for more than Church folk?

2. What do you make logically of the 2$^{nd}$ to last paragraph in the context of the article's general sweep?

3. What is your take on the quotation from Dallas Willard; sense or nonsense and why, either way?

# Article 5

## DEFENDING AND DISMANTLING THE BUGGERY LAW SLOPPILY

**Gist**: At once defending and correcting two clergy colleagues on the buggery law

Two respected clergy colleagues have gone public in support of decriminalizing buggery. These are my former UTCWI lecturer in Psychology, Dr. Howard Gregory, Anglican Lord Bishop of Jamaica, and my JTS classmate and former boss, Dr. Garnett Roper, President of the Jamaica Theological Seminary.

While I disagree with aspects of their stance I think it useful to point out a few crucial things. The first has to do with a distinction between arguing for decriminalization and being in support of a

## SOCIAL ISSUES

decriminalized behaviour or act. The online legal dictionary (Oxford) sees decriminalization as "[t]he process of removing criminal sanctions from any activity either by removing any prohibition of the activity or by moving responsibility for enforcement to a non-criminal process."

It may help to point out that the idea of a **crime** (not simply an offence) is at the heart of decriminalization; hence getting a speeding ticket is an offence in law but not a crime, but robbery, like murder is a crime.

So, the only sure logical conclusion that can be drawn about my two colleagues or anyone else arguing for decriminalization of the act of buggery, is that they do not think it should be a **criminal** act. It does not follow, **without knowing more**, that they support the act of buggery as being amoral (neither right nor wrong in and of itself). We all need to think critically and be fair to others whose views we may not share.

To be sure an act that is decriminalized now could over time be legalized. Bear in mind too that a legal act or practice could be immoral; compare slavery or double taxation by successive political regimes in Jamaica!

## A CONTROVERSIAL CLERGYMAN

Adultery used to be both criminal and immoral. I suspect that not a few persons are happy that it is decriminalized (no longer a criminal act)!

It is also important to know that law and morality don't always overlap, though at times they do. Here is where I disagree somewhat with my dear friend Dr. Roper. He is quoted, arising from a TVJ show called *That's a Rap* as urging that:

> Buggery/anal sex is a moral matter that is between consenting persons; it is a choice which I do not approve of, but that does not make it a criminal act, and what the... 1864 law (Section 61 of the Offences Against the Person Act) does is to make it criminal with a maximum punishment of ten years in prison...

I would suggest to him that buggery in Jamaica is at once a moral **and a criminal** matter. Saying it ***ought not to be*** a criminal matter is radically different from saying it is not a criminal matter when there is a law against it.

Notice though, lest we be sloppy in our reading of Dr. Roper, that he says that "[buggery] is a choice which I do not approve of..."

To the average 'person in the street' it's only a very thin, almost invisible line that separates support for

## SOCIAL ISSUES

decriminalization from support of a decriminalized behaviour or act. For such persons, what is deemed as not criminal is regarded as implicitly okay for behaviour.

This is not so for lawyers though, or for the non-lawyer who is thinking critically. As Dr. Roper's comment shows, one can argue for decriminalization of an act but still find the act unworthy of one's support.

Why do I disagree with Bishop Gregory? His pivots for decriminalization, namely, privacy, consensuality and age-maturity, do not sufficiently justify any sexual behaviour, without more, as the lawyers would say.

The same questionable pivots could be used for incest and other non-sexual acts that are still unlawful. Additionally, buggery must be evaluated intrinsically (what it is in itself). Is it the kind of act/behaviour that a society concerned with individual and societal health should encourage? I don't think so.

Would that religious centres encourage critical thinking and feedback during the weekly worship experiences!

Observer, 30/7/17; Gleaner 5/8/17

# DISCUSSION QUESTIONS

1. How is the author's attempted correction of Dr. Roper not simply nitpicking?

2. How defensible is his criticism of Dr. Gregory?

3. What is the level of clarity you gained about the distinction between decriminalization and legalization from the article?

# Article 6

## ARCHBISHOP JOHN HOLDER ON SODOM/GOMORRAH AND MODERN SODOMY LAWS

**Gist**: The Bajan cleric's views are challenged

Either the newspapers did the esteemed scholar and Anglican prelate, the Most Reverend Dr. John Holder, a disservice in the reports on his presentation at the recently concluded Intimate Conviction conference at UWI or else my senior colleague could have better nuanced, slices of his presentation <u>as</u> reported in the newspapers.

I was not able to attend the conference and tried unsuccessfully to procure a copy of his script or an adequate audio recording of it. I wrote to one of the conference organizers and she referred me to YouTube, but the clip I saw of my brother's presentation was too brief to be useful for analysis.

Before I venture a critical comment on what I read in the newspapers, let it be clear that the situation with me and Dr. Holder is like a sprat questioning a shark, because he has an earned terminal degree in Old Testament studies (Ph.D.) and I have no earned terminal degree in anything!

Dr. Holder allegedly said, "My argument is that using the story of Sodom and Gomorrah to support the sodomy law has no basis, none whatsoever."

Anyone who attempts to appeal to the Sodom and Gomorrah account (15th century BC) to support a modern sodomy law would not be smart, but the Archbishop no doubt has encountered such folk.

I was puzzled though when he allegedly suggested that something is wrong with seeing homosexual behaviour as condemned in the Bible, especially in the Sodom/Gomorrah account.

Based on textual analysis of the Sodom/Gomorrah incident (Gen. 18:16 to 19:29) I share the traditional view that the sin of Sodom and Gomorrah, depicted so graphically in the passage, is homosexuality.

I did not see enough in the papers to tell me what the esteemed Archbishop saw as the moral trigger

## SOCIAL ISSUES

for the punishment of the twin cities, but I know that some scholars see that trigger as inhospitality. In my considered view this position is textually indefensible.

The words of John Boswell in his 1980 book *Christianity, Social Tolerance, and Homosexuality* is representative of this view. Boswell informs:

> When the men of Sodom gathered around to demand that the strangers be brought out to them, 'that they might know them,' they meant no more than to 'know' who they were, and the city was consequently destroyed not for sexual immorality, but for the sin of inhospitality to strangers. (p. 93)

In the text under consideration (Gen. 19) 'to know' is, contextually, sexual, when used concerning the visitors (v.5) and also when Lot used it concerning his daughters who "have not known a man" (v.8).

To appreciate the weakness or nonsense of Boswell's interpretation of 'to know' as 'to interview or interrogate,' try substituting that expression for 'to know' in vs. 5-9. On Boswell's view those verses would read, using the KJV text as our base.

> 5 And they called to Lot and said to him, "Where are the men who came to you tonight?

# A CONTROVERSIAL CLERGYMAN

Bring them out to us that we may **interview them**."

6 So Lot went out to them through the doorway, shut the door behind him,

7 and said, "Please, my brethren, do not do so wickedly!

8 "See now, I have two daughters who **have not interviewed** a man; please, let me bring them out to you, and you may do to them as you wish; only do nothing to these men, since this is the reason they have come under the shadow of my roof."

9 And they said, "Stand back!" Then they said, "This one came in to stay here, and he keeps acting as a judge; now we will deal worse with you than with them."

Right after the men of Sodom express their intention to know the visitors, Lot begs them not to act wickedly. Is Lot silly to regard a mere interview as wicked? And why offer his daughters to the men of Sodom when they really needed to know, according to Boswell, who the strangers were? And what worse were they planning for Lot than what they had in mind for the visitors? An interview mixed with severe physical blows?

It is beyond controversy that hospitality is an issue in the narrative. But it is also beyond controversy that inhospitality was not the central sin of the men in Sodom. Their central sin was homosexuality or attempted homosexual gang rape of Lot's male guests.

One cannot overlook the point that before the alleged 'inhospitality' incident in Gen. 19, it was God's expressed intention in Gen. 18:20ff to destroy Sodom and Gomorrah for their grave sin. Of course, this could be ongoing and aggravated inhospitality or ongoing and aggravated homosexuality. Of those two live options, only homosexuality is regarded as a capital offence in the Old Testament.

The testimony concerning Sodom and Gomorrah elsewhere in the Bible suggests they were guilty of several offences, but the most consistent witness re these cities in the New Testament has to do with sexual immorality.

Jude v.7 says, "just as Sodom and Gomorrah and the cities around them, since they in the same way as these indulged in gross immorality and went after strange flesh, are exhibited as an example in undergoing the punishment of eternal fire."

2 Pet. 2:7,8 and 10 say of Lot in Sodom, "(... for [he] was oppressed by the sensual conduct of unprincipled men...by what he saw and heard that righteous man, while living among them, felt his righteous soul tormented day after day by their lawless deeds...)"

Whatever other sin is involved in the Sodom and Gomorrah narrative in Genesis, homosexuality heads the list.

Gleaner, 18/10/17 (as 'Forming the Ass on Sodom')

## DISCUSSION QUESTIONS

1. Does the author's admission that he lacks an earned doctorate put him in an unenviable position argumentatively, *vis-à-vis* the Archbishop and why or why not?

2. Why isn't the author guilty of the strawman fallacy (re the Archbishop) in his critique of Boswell's views on the Sodom/Gomorrah narrative?

3. How do you arbitrate when two specialists disagree on a point?

# Article 7

## LEGAL PHILOSOPHER JOHN FINNIS ON HOMOSEXUALITY

**Gist**: A critique of a *Gleaner* editorial on a challenge to Jamaica's 'buggery law'

The *Gleaner* editorial of December 11, 2015 wished luck on Human Rights lawyer Maurice Tomlinson's constitutional challenge of Jamaica's 'buggery law' and the editorial went on to treat the objection to homosexual acts as informed primarily, if not exclusively, by an appeal to religious texts. This view from whomever wrote that editorial is almost unpardonably myopic and ignorant of the legal literature. I explain.

John Mitchell Finnis is an Australian legal scholar and philosopher specializing in the philosophy of law. In his essay *"Law, Morality and 'Sexual Orientation"* he cogently shows that it is very possible to argue against homosexual acts without appealing to any religious texts. In the opening section of this fascinating essay (available online), Finnis sums up his position on homosexual activity, which is counter to Mr. Tomlinson's (and the *Gleaner's* editorial) and goes on to say that his position:

> ... involves a number of explicit or implicit judgments about the proper role of law and the compelling interests of political communities, and about the evil of homosexual conduct. **Can these be defended by reflective, critical, publicly intelligible and rational arguments? I believe they can.** The judgment that it is morally wrong need not be a manifestation either of mere hostility to a hated minority, or of purely religious, theological, and sectarian belief. (my emphasis)

Finnis continues, "Let me begin by noticing a too little noticed fact. All three of the greatest Greek philosophers, Socrates, Plato and Aristotle, regarded homosexual conduct as intrinsically shameful, immoral, and indeed depraved or depraving. That is to say, all three rejected the linchpin of modern "gay" ideology and lifestyle. Socrates is portrayed by

Plato (and by Xenophon) as having strong homosexual (as well as heterosexual) inclinations or interest, and as promoting an ideal of homosexual romance between men and youths, but at the same time as utterly rejecting homosexual conduct."

Finnis draws support for his reading of the Greek philosophers from the likes of the late pre-eminent Socratic scholar Gregory Vlastos, and Sir Kenneth Dover, late distinguished Classical scholar, I think precisely because they are, legally speaking, 'hostile witnesses' in that neither agreed with the views of the great Greek philosophers on homosexuality.

Going on, Finnis argues, "Plato saw anal intercourse as 'contrary to nature,' a degradation not only of man's humanity, but even of his animality... a type of act far more serious than any mere going "contrary to the rules". As for Aristotle, there is widespread scholarly agreement that he rejected homosexual conduct. In fact, such conduct is frequently represented by Aristotle (in some cases directly and in other cases by a lecturer's hint) as intrinsically perverse, shameful and harmful both to the individuals involved and to society itself.

> Although the ideology of homosexual love (with its accompanying devaluation of women) continued to have philosophical defenders down to the end of classical Greek civilisation, there equally continued to be influential philosophical

writers, wholly untouched by Judaeo-Christian tradition, who taught that homosexual conduct is not only intrinsically shameful but also inconsistent with a proper recognition of the equality of women with men in intrinsic worth.

(The ancients did not fail to note that Socrates' homoerotic orientation, for all its admirable chastity -- abstention from homosexual conduct -- went along with a neglect to treat his wife as an equal.) A good example of such late classical writing is Plutarch's *Erotikos* (Dialogue on Love)...written probably some time in the early second century, but certainly free from Judaeo-Christian influence.

Another example is the Stoic, Musonius Rufus (who taught at Rome c. 80 AD and again was not influenced by Jewish or Christian thought). He rejects all homosexual conduct as shameful. Sexual conduct is decent and acceptable only within marriage.

All of the above quotations from Finnis are just from the first 5 pages of his stimulating essay. I recommend it highly to all educated Christians, lawyers especially and other thinkers in our society.

Mr. Tomlinson will need much more than luck if his constitutional challenge is to pass philosophico-legal muster. [Gleaner 16/12/15]

# SOCIAL ISSUES

## DISCUSSION QUESTIONS

1. In what way or to what extent is the author's use of Finnis useful, logically?

2. Mr. Tomlinson, in response to this article, chided Finnis' views as from a devout religious man. Fair or unfair chiding, and why either way?

3. Given the legal taboo on anal intercourse, why shouldn't a free society be required to provide a defence of what it regards as lawful sexual intercourse?

# Part II

# SOCIETAL CONCERNS

# Article 8

## WHAT'S SO WRONG WITH...IF?

**Gist**: A mischievous challenge to think more critically about societal ills

Weeks ago when I read the allegation that some Police Officers were being overlooked for promotion because they refused the sexual advances of superior colleagues, I smiled mischievously, saying to myself philosophically 'so what's so wrong with requesting or demanding sex for promotion...?' A similar thing happens to me when I hear or read of the societal furore about corruption, scamming, etc., etc.

# A CONTROVERSIAL CLERGYMAN

Careless Christian readers of the above who are tempted to write me off as backslidden or unsaved should know that I couldn't care less, because none of you has access to the 'Lamb's book of life'.

What's so wrong with any so-called ill in Jamaica if our preferred ethical principle and practice is relativism, the belief that there are no absolutes so everything depends on the situation or circumstance surrounding an act or intention to act?

Two months ago I started a series in our circuit of churches with the title of this article minus the "if", and we began with and are still on gambling and hope to go on to premarital and extramarital sex. I hope to help our people develop critical thinking on issues of practical importance to all of our lives.

If there is really no such thing as 'always right or always wrong' with reference to acts or intentions to act, then our moral outrage at whatever is empty, though we may not realize it philosophically.

A few years ago, while I was still in Florida, there was a major exam cheating scandal at the University of Central Florida which outraged the University bigwigs and the wider community. Philosophical mischief seized me, and the morning after the scandal was aired on the nightly TV news I called the University and asked the person who answered what the fuss was all about, and more so 'what's so wrong

## SOCIETAL CONCERNS

with cheating on a University exam?' The lady on the phone was adamant that it was wrong and I calmly kept on asking why. She just stopped short of calling me a morally bankrupt fool and then I asked her which University lecturer there believed in or taught any ethical viewpoint beside relativism.

I have encouraged Christian students to request from the authorities a reason why they monitor every single exam to ensure that no one ever cheats. Why, if the default ethical viewpoint is that there is no such thing as always right and always wrong? If relativism rules, why not allow each student to cheat at least only on the most important exam of his/her academic career as determined by the student?

Here is the rub. There is a delightful flexibility and fluidity about ethical relativism, and it appeals to the basic desire for ethical autonomy (self-rule) that we all register at the core of our beings. Yes, even religious folk.

If the rightness or wrongness of an act is determined by me, then I become the final court of appeal concerning the ethical value to be put on that act. That is delightful in principle and in practice, or so it seems. Ponder a few scenarios.

Declaring as true what one knows or suspects is false, i.e. lying, has no intrinsic ethical status for the consistent relativist. The existential context in which

## A CONTROVERSIAL CLERGYMAN

one tells a lie is what allows a value judgement to be made on the declaration.

Converting to one's use and benefit funds belonging to another, without the authority or permission so to do, i.e. stealing or fraud, has no intrinsic ethical status for the consistent relativist. The existential context in which one does the act is what allows a value judgement to be made on the converting.

Pre-marital, extra-marital or homosexual sex has no intrinsic ethical status for the consistent relativist. The existential context in which one engages in sexual intimacy is what allows a value judgement to be made on the act of intimacy.

At the level of ethical practice, ethical relativism is delightful to live on, but uncomfortable to live with. If I am ethically free to indulge my desires, then every other person is entitled to that luxury, even to my detriment. Work with this half-crazy parson a bit more.

If ethical relativism is defensible, then the consistent relativist could not instinctively or belatedly experience or express outrage at any so-called 'wrong,' because it could be right owing to the context in which it happened. Rob the relativist, swindle him in business, rape or seduce his wife, bugger his son, lie on him in Court, etc., and he would be forced to grin and bear it because any such act could be right.

Why then the ethical furore over non-transparency in the awarding of fat governmental contracts if relativism rules? Why the moral outrage concerning realities in our country: companies that use double-invoicing to evade the tax man, contract murders, cheating in exams, evading customs, multiple-taxation laws, sex for promotion, etc., if relativism rules and is defensible as a principle of ethical decision-making?

There are negative societal spin-offs of ethical relativism. There is no easy way of seeing how ethical relativism can curb human desires that are or could be detrimental to a business or a community. Nor is it conceivable that ethical relativism could inculcate a sense of ethical duty or the sense of 'ought' in anyone.

Even relativists recognize and admit to this defect in ethical relativism. Humanist and ethical relativist, Paul Kurtz writes:

> ...the humanist is faced with a crucial ethical problem: Insofar as he has defended an ethic of freedom, can he develop a basis for moral responsibility? Regretfully, merely to liberate individuals from authoritarian social

institutions, whether church or state, is no guarantee that they will be aware of their moral responsibility to others. The contrary is often the case. (Cited in David Noebel, *Understanding the Times*, p. 206)

And yet, despite the fact that at the level of ethical practice, ethical relativism is delightful to live on but uncomfortable to live with, absolutism may be delightful to live with but extremely difficult to live on consistently.

Observer 8/10/17

# DISCUSSION QUESTIONS

1. Honestly, what was your instinctive initial response after reading the article?

2. How logically compelling did you find the article? Cite sections.

3. Where was the weakest logical point in the article and why?

# Article 9

## PLAYING DEADLY GAMES WITH TOBACCO

**Gist**: A call to connect the dots between societal knowledge and practice

The recent 'World No Tobacco Day' left me a tad puzzled. If the multiple warnings from the WHO and similar organisations about the health dangers of tobacco smoking are scientifically sound, why are governments cat-walking around the issue by simply increasing taxation on cigarettes and demanding better warning labels?

How about progressive legislation toward the elimination of the tobacco industry re smoking?

Unrealistic, idealistic? Maybe, but are we realistic in thinking that increased taxation on tobacco products is really different from benefiting from the proceeds of a crime against humanity? Like seriously?

So we think better warning labels will make a greater dent in the attractiveness of cigarettes to youngsters and others? Who is kidding whom? How about working overtime towards making the deadly product unavailable?

If you are concerned about protecting the rights of smokers to do what they choose with their own bodies do bear in mind the effects of 2nd hand smoke on other people's bodies.

So again, if the health warnings about second hand smoke are scientifically sound, smokers are being allowed (by a rights argument) to be, at once, suicidal and homicidal. Would any defender of such rights stand up in a serious debate or in a Court of law and argue this kind of case?

Alas, humanity seems to be progressively diminishing the claim to be called *homo sapiens* (wise or sensible human) and is sliding towards being called *homo saps* (eediat [idiotic] human)!

Observer letter 5/6/16

## DISCUSSION QUESTIONS

1. The letter is concise, but how cogent was the author's argumentation?

2. Would you expect any governmental body to do anything about the author's recommendation; why or why not?

3. Did the letter affect your view on tobacco use and if so, how so?

# Article 10

## UNPALATABLE FOOD FOR THOUGHT

**Gist**: Probing the root cause of crime while disabusing minds of the panacea of more and better policing

Everybody ought to know that even if Jamaica had enough money and police/soldier personnel in the millions, crime and violence would not thereafter be eradicated.

The Police and soldiers who seek to curb wrongdoing are necessary but most definitely not sufficient even to reduce crime dramatically, because trite though it sounds, it is incontestably true that

## SOCIETAL CONCERNS

the heart of our crime problem is a problem of the heart of people.

Even the most rabidly irreligious and erudite Psychiatrist would be hard-pressed to rebut, let alone refute, the notion in an ancient 7$^{th}$ century BCE Jewish religious text in Hebrew which says "the heart is deceitful above all things and desperately wicked, who can know it?" or differently translated, "The heart is more deceitful than anything else and incurable—who can understand it?"

All or most of us have been at times puzzled by the awful nature of our inner inclinations to act and our actual actions, and so we all can verify the truthfulness of the very old maxim of that religious text.

Ponder this hypothetical scenario. What if, one night, after sleeping with my wife for the past 42 years, I decide, God forbid, to strangle her to death in her sleep? Which police or soldier would even be near to block me? The pre-crime division of the movie Minority Report is still only fiction!

Even when we strengthen our legislation and enforcement mechanisms, we still must reckon with the largely unpredictable human psyche/soul/heart which makes mockery of our wishes at preventing/reducing crime!

## A CONTROVERSIAL CLERGYMAN

Concerning the power of laws, the sage words of the Scottish patriot Andrew Fletcher come to mind: "Let me write the songs of a nation and I care not who makes its laws." Laws, whether divine or human in origin, are only external regulators of conduct, but they are incapable of helping any of us to avoid the wrong and do the right!

Should we not then show real concern about transforming the hearts/psyches of our people while we increase Zones of Special Operation and States of Emergency?

Observer 18/10/18

## DISCUSSION QUESTIONS

1. Is this veiled pessimism or blind optimism and why either way?

2. Comment critically on the argumentative value of the scenario the author has in paragraph 5.

3. Research crime in some of the 'safest countries' in the world and develop an argument to counter or justify the author's closing question.

# Article 11

## HOW RELIGION POISONS EVERYTHING

**Gist**: A logical chiding of a critic of religion

I chose the headline of this column (reflected here) because it is the subtitle of a book that forms the springboard for my reflection now.

The late, notorious atheist Christopher Hitchens published a best-seller titled *God Is Not Great: How Religion Poisons Everything*.

The book is well written, but his case is very poorly argued. The subtitle is far too ambitious thus making proof of the thesis well-nigh impossible. Philosophically, the term 'everything' in the subtitle means that nothing at all escapes the poisonous impact of religion (Christianity included and Christianity especially).

Hitchens' atheistic forerunner, the German Philosopher Friedrich Nietzsche, made a similar blunder in his book *The Antichrist*, when he said:

> I condemn Christianity. I raise against the Christian church the most terrible accusation that any accuser has ever uttered. It is to me the ultimate conceivable corruption. It has possessed the will to the final corruption that is even possible. **The Christian church has left nothing untouched by its depravity:** it has turned every value into a disvalue, every truth into a falsehood, every integrity into a vileness of the soul. (my emphasis)

This is almost unpardonable coming from a professional philosopher, an excessive indictment minus supporting evidence.

If the thesis of these two atheists is even roughly or partially true, then when we flit through the annals of history over any given period it should be difficult to find anything praiseworthy about Christianity's impact on society, since according to Hitchens it poisons not just a few or some things but everything (bar nothing) and according to Nietzsche it has left nothing untouched by its depravity. Are you with me?

As I hammer home with my philosophy students, 'try to avoid extreme words and phrases, use loophole language.' All Hitchens had to do was say religion poisons almost everything and take refuge from Christian critics in the qualifier 'almost.' Similarly, Nietzsche would be less exposed philosophically had he said, 'almost nothing.'

Forget for the time being raising questions with Hitchens or Nietzsche about the irredeemable badness/wrongness of poisoning or touching with depravity [anything or everything] and the moral yardstick that they, as atheists, are using to declare anything bad, wrong or depraved!

Though it is tempting to indulge a protracted tangent and show up the worldview blind spots here, I shall resist the temptation but encourage you in your own musings or dialogue with an atheist to raise these kinds of issues.

I want to show you now why Hitchens' central claim, like Nietzsche's, is patently false by giving you just a few tidbits of the Church's Impact on Western civilization.

Every student of world history ought to know, but some don't know, of the Church's pioneering work in societies. As the US Christian lawyer Craig Parton says, the world is still waiting for the first leper colony founded by an atheist.

The evidence of voluntary charity and compassion seen in the rise of orphanages, homes for the aged, the Salvation Army, the various Catholic groups like Sisters of Charity and Missionaries of the Poor, United Way, YMCA, YWCA, Teen Challenge, hospitals, mental institutions, the Red Cross/Red Crescent/Red Lion and numerous other agencies for the care of needy human beings can be traced back to the Church of Jesus Christ.

Consider the Church's role in education. Churches provided education for slaves and both sexes. Martin Luther (1483-1546) was behind tax-supported public schools and compulsory education. Lutheran layman Johann Sturm (1507-1589) pioneered graded education. Three French Christians in the 18th century championed the cause of education for the deaf. Louis Braille in the 19th century pioneered education for the blind.

The oldest and most prestigious universities in the world had Christian roots; check the history of the University of Bologna, the University of Paris, Oxford, Cambridge, Harvard, Princeton, Yale, Heidelberg and Columbia, etc.

## SOCIETAL CONCERNS

For those (especially degreed professionals) who have a problem with the probative value of the Bible I mention the fact that several legal luminaries in history, and a few still with us, have cross-examined some of the documents of the Bible and adjudged them reliable. A modern lawyer in Jamaica now would be extremely pride-filled to say that he/she is the intellectual equal of the names I'll mention now.

Hugh Grotius of the 16th century (regarded as the father of international law); Sir Matthew Hale of the 17th century (Lord High Chancellor under Charles II); William Blackstone (who codified English common law in the 18th century); Simon Greenleaf (Dean of the Harvard Law School of the 19th century); Lord Hailsham (former Lord High Chancellor in the 20th century) and John Warwick Montgomery (English Barrister and American attorney, current trial lawyer in human rights cases in the International Court of Human Rights in Strasbourg, France). For these facts and more see Craig Parton's *Religion on Trial: Cross-Examining Religious Truth Claims*, 2018 and his *The Defense Never Rests*, 2015.

Let those who find perverse pleasure in chewing on the dead flesh provided by sinning members of the Church continue to gorge themselves, but let the records reflect that the animus that some have toward the Church and religion cannot attract any

# A CONTROVERSIAL CLERGYMAN

justification when the annals of history are carefully examined.

*Observer* 17/9/18

# DISCUSSION QUESTIONS

1. How has the author justified his broadside against Hitchens and Nietzsche?

2. Evaluate the author's suggestion that an atheist would have problems defending value terms such as 'bad, wrong or depraved.'

3. After double checking the author's historical claims, how would you modify your initial response to question #1?

# Article 12

## ETHICAL LEADERSHIP: DEFINITION AND DEFENSE

**Gist**: Probing the implications of a call for an ethics campaign from Custos Bishop Conrad Pitkin

Custos of St. James, Bishop Conrad Pitkin at his installation ceremony on Thursday issued a call for an ethics campaign and according to the *Gleaner's Western Bureau* said: "I pledge that in this office, I will work hand in hand with you to continue instilling strong moral values and attitudes in our children and youth for them to be better-prepared citizens."

# A CONTROVERSIAL CLERGYMAN

This call from the Custos triggered my thoughts on the widespread need for ethical leadership which in my view goes beyond ordinary leadership.

If a leader is basically "a person who influences people to accomplish a purpose," then leadership is the art of influencing people to accomplish a purpose. Critical then to the basic effectiveness of a leader, or the cultivation of basic skills in the art of leadership, would be qualitative development on the leader's part on three dimensions: the person dimension, the people dimension and the purpose dimension.

It should be clear that by this basic and traditional approach to leadership there is nothing clearly stated or even implied about the nature of the end in view. Similarly, there is nothing clearly stated or even implied about the nature of the means that will be employed to achieve the end in view.

Based on this approach, Adolph Hitler and Mother Teresa were and are equally deserving of compliments as successful and effective leaders even though their purposes and means were radically different.

My working definition of ethical leadership then is "the net result of the power of a life lived consistently on high ethical principles impacting positively on

## SOCIETAL CONCERNS

other lives and influencing them to accomplish a wholesome purpose."

Related and implied terms: *integrity and character*

Integrity is 'abiding fidelity to wholesome, abiding principles,' and borders on being an absolute.

The awful reality is that, unless leaders in the private and public sectors reflect a commitment in principle and in practice to wholesome abiding principles, a society pays a high ethical price—trust will be killed or gravely wounded by cynicism and skepticism, corruption will become almost endemic and national development will be delayed. A few quotes from two Jamaicans and a foreigner should help.

> Where there are no high ethical standards, the cost attached to malpractices in public life becomes trivial...The values of the society are fundamentally changing, and hustling, rackets and scams are now considered as normal activity provided you make sure that you are not caught. [Professor Carl Stone, *Daily Gleaner*, 7/12/92]

> What we are facing today is not a crisis of economic stability, we are getting there; this is

not a crisis of courage, we have the strength; this is a crisis of conscience, character and the inner spirit of man. [Dennis Lalor, Daily Gleaner, 13/12/92]

During the last century, man cast off the fetters of religion. Hardly was he free, however, when he created new and utterly intolerable chains...The kingdom of grace has been conquered, but the kingdom of justice is crumbling too. Europe is dying of this disappointing realization.[ Albert Camus, *The Rebel*, 1956, 279-280]

*Character*, as its Greek roots suggest, is the mark engraved or impressed on a coin or seal and so metaphorically, the distinctive mark of a person, the core or essential 'stuff' of a person, which could be either good or bad. As Os Guinness says, character "...is the indelible stamp on a person beneath all masks, poses, disguises, and social veneers...[it] is what we are when no one sees but God." (*When No One Sees: The Importance of Character in an Age of Image*, 2000, p.16). Put differently character is 'what we are when not acting under the pressure of profiling.'

## SOCIETAL CONCERNS

### Character vs. Image

Character is like the stuff that goes into the building of a solid reinforced concrete wall. It is being good in essence (Gk. *agathos*)

*Image* is like the attractive veneer of wood carefully painted to look like a concrete wall. It is simply 'looking good' (Gk. *kalos*)

Ethical leaders are more concerned about character than image!!

When character takes priority over image it fosters certain crucial leadership characteristics like:

*Commitment* (openness to taking on and completing tasks agreed on as necessary for individual or group development)

*Persistence* (the ability to overcome obstacles while pursuing noble goals)

*Self-Mastery* (marked by a degree of discipline and self-control)

Wholesome character in leadership is absolutely fundamental. The fruit called public leadership and the fruit called private life spring from the same root—character.

> ...Character in leaders is important for two key reasons. Externally, character provides the

point of trust that links leaders with followers. Internally, character is the part-gyroscope, part-brake that provides the leader's deepest source of bearings and strongest source of restraint. In many instances the first prompting to do good and the last barrier against doing wrong are the same—character. (Guinness, op. cit., p. 26)

It is not an exaggeration to say that the wellspring of ethical leadership is character, with integrity as the initial evidence of character's presence. Nor is it an exaggeration to say that the malaise now afflicting and affecting Jamaican leaders in all spheres of the society is the other AIDS virus—Acquired Integrity Deficiency Syndrome. (This twist on AIDS as an acronym is borrowed from Gene Antonio, *The AIDS Cover-up? The Real and Alarming Facts About AIDS*, 1987, p.141).

Integrity deficiency is itself an indication of the need for transformation at the level of character. We can only hope Bishop Pitkin's call will be heeded.

Gleaner & Observer, 11/4/18

SOCIETAL CONCERNS

# DISCUSSION QUESTIONS

1. How realistic is the call of the Custos?

2. What practical insights, if any, did you glean from the article?

3. Can the enterprise of values and attitudes really succeed, and why either way?

# Article 13

# THE KNOWLEDGE VS. BELIEF CONFUSION

**Gist**: Clarifying a very popular view about the topic

It is too widespread a confusion for me to leave it unchallenged. I am talking about the claim that belief is inferior to knowledge (without more, as lawyers would say).

Michael Abrahams' column in the *Gleaner* yesterday (July 9, 2018) betrayed this confusion and I had to deal with it in passing in a public forum at UTECH in 2001 involving Dr. Leahcim Semaj and Mutabaruka.

Every statement purporting to be fact or true is a belief. Indeed, if you call to mind the basic moods in

## SOCIETAL CONCERNS

English language sentences, then if it is not a question (interrogative mood), a command (imperative mood), a wish (subjunctive mood), then it is in the indicative mood (an assertion, claiming something). Every such assertion or claim qualifies as a belief, but since some beliefs are quite reasonable and some are unreasonable we need to probe further.

In philosophy, the basic understanding is that ***knowledge is justified or warranted belief***. So, knowledge is a species of belief!

Indeed, there is another dimension that some philosophers add concerning knowledge:

> [I]f someone knows something then what he knows must be true...so a necessary condition of knowledge is that what is known is true. But truth is not sufficient [adequate] for knowledge. There are many truths that no one has ever thought of, much less known. And there are some truths that someone may think about but not know. (J.P. Moreland & William Craig, *Philosophical Foundations for a Christian Worldview*, 2003, pages 71 and 73).

If I say I believe something, that claim is not inferior to another person's claim to know that same thing, because there is no necessary doubt in the statement "I believe X," neither is there necessary certainty in the statement "I know X." In both cases justification or warrant is needed to make the claim reasonable or justified/warranted belief.

This can be a humbug for most of us. For instance, in my home church where I was a member with my family (after resigning my first pastorate), I was asked to preach near Easter Sunday and chided the popular song *"He Lives,"* especially the section that says, "You ask me how I know He lives, He lives within my heart." For me that is useful only if you need subjective assurance. It is not helpful if you wish to convince someone else about the living reality of Jesus.

In my usual Q & A time after a sermon, a dear sister defended the stanza I took to task by emphasizing how much it meant to her in her personal life. I applauded her but still emphasized the need for more than the subjective even for self and especially for others. When we share about Jesus with others they have a right to demand justification or warrant for our belief in Jesus as whomever/whatever to us.

The people that I have served over the years as Pastor know what I remind them about regularly, that "I am half crazy" and will do unconventional things as a preacher-teacher in the pulpit, like asking questions of the congregation and prompting them

## SOCIETAL CONCERNS

to ask me questions about what I shared (time allowing). If learning is the name of the game, then dialogue between the pew and the pulpit is critical to that enterprise.

Free thinkers (non-theists, atheists, agnostics, deists, and others) need to understand as well that when they make bold claims about their views on God and religion, they too must provide justification or warrant for what they believe or claim to know.

The burden of proof is always primarily on the one who makes a claim or asserts something.

Observer 7/8/18

# DISCUSSION QUESTIONS

1. What would you say as a judge of the logic of the article?

2. In what particular(s) did you identify with the author's points?

3. Did the writer challenge your thinking or appeal to your emotions and how so either way?

# Article 14

## AN ABORTION PRIMER

**Gist**: Critical thinking pointers for the abortion dialogue

When thinking critically about aborting or terminating a pregnancy one needs to ask and attempt to answer a few fundamental questions prior to moving toward a tentative or final informed decision.

The most central one, in my view, is dealt with here.

1. Fundamental Question and Answer: What is the unborn within a pregnant woman?

Scientifically, the offspring of a species cannot be other than a member of that species, therefore, the unborn is, unquestionably, a human being, *Homo sapiens*.

> So, therefore, it is scientifically correct to say that an individual human life begins at conception, when egg and sperm join to form the zygote, and this developing human always is a member of our species in all stages of its life. (Dr. Micheline Matthews-Roth, Department of Medicine, Harvard Medical School, cited in Francis J. Beckwith, *Politically Correct Death: Answering Arguments for Abortion Rights*, 1993, 43)

It is instructive that in their report to the U.S. Senate Judiciary Committee (1981), the U.S. Senate subcommittee made the telling comment that:

> No witness [who testified before the subcommittee] raised any evidence to refute the biological fact that from the moment of conception there exists a distinct individual being who is alive and is of the human species. No witness challenged the scientific consensus that unborn children are 'human beings'... (Cited in Beckwith, op. cit., 43. See also Bradley Patten, *Human Embryology*, 1968, 43; E.L. Potter et al, *Pathology of the Fetus and the Infant*, 1975, vii; Keith L. Moore, *The*

*Developing Human: Clinically Oriented Embryology*, 1977, 12)

As Christian Apologist Greg Koukl has argued, if the unborn is not a human being, no justification is necessary to kill it. If the unborn is an innocent human being, almost no justification is adequate for killing it. Any reason advanced for killing the innocent unborn human being, he argues, should be tested against the question, 'would it be justifiable to kill any other human being **for the same reason**?'

There is hardly any serious debate now (legally, ethically, medically) about the humanity, personhood and innocence of the unborn, so the debate turns largely on the desire/wish of the pregnant woman to terminate her pregnancy or kill the innocent unborn human within her womb.

Now Koukl's test question above raises the issue of justifiable homicide [killing a human being]. In law, I gather, not all killings qualify as murder, so we have justifiable homicide. As a lawyer advised me, if an armed intruder threatens your life and property and you respond by killing that one, that homicide, in law, would be justified.

So, one could attempt an argument for abortion as justifiable homicide. One philosopher, Judith Jarvis Thompson has done precisely that in her provocative 1986 essay *'Unplugging the Violinist.'*

## SOCIETAL CONCERNS

In this essay she uses a story to make a point in defence of a woman's right to an abortion even if one concedes the personhood, humanity and innocence of the unborn.

Thompson asks readers to imagine waking up one morning and finding yourself back to back with an unconscious famous violinist who has a life-threatening liver condition and after intensive research of medical records you have been identified as the only person with the right blood type to help.

So, friends of his in the musical fraternity arranged for your kidnapping and arranged for the violinist's circulatory system to be plugged into yours, thus your kidneys do double duty, extracting poisons from his blood and yours. To unplug you from him would be to kill him. Good news though, the process is only for nine months by which time he would have improved sufficiently to be safely unplugged from you.

Thompson's argument is impressive but not beyond refutation. Philosopher Francis J. Beckwith says "[t]here (sic.) at least nine problems with Thompson's argument. These problems can be put into three categories: ethical, legal and ideological." (op. cit., 129)

I'll isolate only one of Beckwith's problems with Thompson's argument but, for me, being forced to have someone plugged into you is radically different from, and so not analogous with, becoming pregnant (rape aside) after a consensual and thus volitional unprotected sex act which a woman would know ahead of time (based on her menstrual cycle) could probably result in pregnancy.

Beckwith urges the point that "Thompson's argument is fatal to family morality...which [suggests] that an individual has special and filial obligations to his offspring and family that he does not have to other persons."

Thus, the unborn "does have a *prima facie* right (though not an absolute natural claim) to her mother's body, [unlike Thompson's violinist who is artificially attached to another person and is therefore not naturally dependent on any particular human being], for this is how human beings are at this stage of their development."

This period of a human being's natural development occurs in the womb...and is a necessary condition for any human being's post-uterine existence... the womb is the unborn's natural environment, whereas being artificially hooked up to a stranger is not the natural environment for the violinist...the unborn [thus] has a *prima facie* natural claim upon her mother's body. (130, 131)

## SOCIETAL CONCERNS

It is not just merely possible but probable or likely that a brighter-than-Beckwith local pro-choice lawyer or philosopher can debunk Beckwith, thereby providing invaluable class discussion and exam material for those of us who teach philosophy, ethics or related subjects. Just a critical thinking **primer** for the abortion debate.

Observer 24/5/18, Gleaner 27/5/18

## DISCUSSION QUESTIONS

1. In what way did the author appeal to your mind as opposed to your emotions?

2. What did you learn that you did not know before reading the article?

3. What was the author's purpose/motive in mentioning Thompson's article?

# Article 15

## OF ILLEGAL DRUGS, GUNS AND SEX

**Gist**: Very provocative suggestions on the topic

Two non-Jamaican writers have made statements that still have impact on my mind. Concerning the drug epidemic in the USA, decades ago Dr. A.E. Wilder-Smith, a Christian academic, said the root cause is not so much the physical availability of drugs to people but the psychical availability of people to drugs.

He urged the supporting point that, whereas inhabitants of the major poppy-growing regions of the world rarely become heroin addicts, the USA was reeling from heroin addiction!

I think Wilder-Smith's sage suggestion re illicit drugs has relevance for us in Jamaica and it applies equally to our problem with illicit guns. Our psychical availability to unwholesome things and behaviours is largely neglected by societal thinkers and planners. We may not be able to radicalize the national mindset on some things but that is no reason to give up on trying.

There are many Jamaicans of all stripes who cannot at all be pulled into the web of illicit guns and/or drugs because of who they are psychically.

This psychic state of being that makes some of them unavailable to things unlawful may not have anything to do with religion either! In fact, if one has only a mild dose of religion rather than the real 'disease', psychical unavailability to things unlawful is not guaranteed at all.

The vulnerability of a given Parson, Police person, Politician or any other Jamaican to things unlawful is largely influenced by the state of that one's essential being (character) and values, but this dimension is too often neglected in social analyses of criminality and corruption in Jamaica.

The other non-Jamaican writer whose ideas I have in mind here has a strange surname which has

# A CONTROVERSIAL CLERGYMAN

slipped my mature mind now. He was arguing the point that "your response is your responsibility," a troubling notion if you are hooked on the traditional approach to stimulus and response.

So, when I blame folk for making me do X, Y or Z, I ought to reckon with the fact, the writer suggests, that I am the kind of person that responds a certain way to certain stimuli. Taking his approach, while the force of the stimulus is not disregarded, the focus is more on the one responding.

He used a most insightful illustration of his point by saying that a grain of sand in the human eye is most irritating but a few grains of sand in an oyster gives rise to a pearl. If the focus should be on the stimulus then we could expect even the odd pearl when sand gets in our eye. It's the oyster's makeup (character) that makes the sand-pearl phenomenon even possible.

So apply that illustration to the realm of sexual temptation. It is not so much the aesthetic potentialities of that lady's face/body or attire that make me think of stalking her, or that prompt me to sexually harass, assault or sleep with her but, I am **the kind of person (character wise)** who responds the way I do.

Uncomfortable though the thought is "my response is my responsibility."

## SOCIETAL CONCERNS

Sitting at ease within ourselves with self-control, though difficult to attain/maintain, is always the best antidote against being psychically available for the unlawful and/or the immoral. A person's reach might exceed that one's grasp, but the intention and effort are worth it.

Observer 14/10/18, Gleaner 16/10/18

## DISCUSSION QUESTIONS

1. Which is the most challenging paragraph for you? Identify and offer your critique of it?

2. What in the article do you agree with logically but wish to reject practically and why?

3. In what way is the sand in the eye vs. in an oyster illustration a logical move or leap?

# Article 16

## THE 'OWN BODY ARGUMENT': SENSE AND NONSENSE

**Gist**: Challenging a popular pro-choice argument

The people who favour abortion are correct. A pregnant woman should have the right to decide what happens to her own body. However, we should not go on and talk nonsense beyond that statement which needs proper nuancing.

At a common-sense level, it should be remembered that no one at all has any unchallengeable right to do what s(he) pleases with that one's own body. You are forbidden by law to attempt to kill yourself or do serious harm to your own body with intent to commit suicide. What of indecent exposure laws also?

## SOCIETAL CONCERNS

Given seat belt and helmet laws, are drivers (at least) free to do what they like with their own bodies in/on a moving vehicle? Then what of the current sugary drinks hype and the possible legal developments?

I say again, no one at all has any unchallengeable right to do what s(he) pleases with that one's own body.

At the deeper technical medical level now, everybody ought to know that the unborn in a pregnant woman's body is not scientifically the pregnant woman's body nor even a part of it! Shocked, surprised? Check out what's below with a trusted health practitioner since I failed Bio at O'Levels.

I did precisely that after reading it in reputable science books and after asking my wife (a Professor of Biology) about it.

The basic scientific reality is that a body part is defined by the common genetic code it shares with the rest of the body to which it belongs.

The genetic code of the unborn is different from the mother's!

A pregnant woman can be injured and die yet her child is delivered alive! Ponder a quotation from the former leading abortionist in the USA, Dr. Bernard Nathanson:

"...the modern science of immunology has shown that the unborn child is not part of a woman's body in the sense that her kidney or heart is." (Bernard Nathanson, in *The Abortion Papers: Inside the Abortion Mentality*, 1983, 150. See his fascinating 1996 book, *The Hand of God*.)

We need to avoid a hugely popular logical blunder. Thinking that being inside or being connected to something means being part of that thing. Consider being connected to a spacecraft in outer space. Think about a mouse in a mint-ball jar; is it a mint-ball or just maybe a sugar-coated mouse?

The so-called 'navel string' or umbilical cord is produced by the unborn and is attached to, and at birth cut from, the placenta (the 'after birth'), which is also produced by the unborn. The 'navel string' is not really attached to the mother at all!

> The placenta is responsible for working as a trading post between the mother's and the baby's blood supply...blood vessels carrying the fetal blood run through the placenta...Nutrients and oxygen from the mother's blood are transferred to the fetal blood... waste products are transferred from the fetal blood to the maternal blood, without the two blood supplies mixing. *(American Pregnancy Association.org)*

Imagine my consternation then, when on *'Balancing Justice'* on RJR (March 19, 2019) I thought I heard my esteemed friend, Gynaecologist Dr. Michael Abrahams, using the 'own body' argument. Owing to my respect for my friend I assumed my old ears were playing tricks on me until I heard the astute Attorney Philippa Davies pointing out to Michael that the unborn was not a part of the pregnant woman's body.

So then, even beyond the need to nuance the 'own body' right notion generally, the argument fails miserably and is nonsense with reference to a pregnant woman.

This fallacious 'own body' argument is really used as a lead-in to the argument of "women's rights" or, to use the code name employed in U.N. declarations "reproductive rights"!

It seems to be largely overlooked that this same U.N. in its Declaration of the Rights of the Child (1950, and again in 1989) stated in the preamble:

"Whereas the child, by reason of his physical and mental immaturity, needs special safeguards and care, including appropriate legal protection, before as well as after birth ..."

Despite how we might feel about issues, let us commit to engaging our critical minds, always.

Gleaner, 3/4/19

## DISCUSSION QUESTIONS

1. In what way did the author appeal to your mind as opposed to your emotions?

2. What did you learn that you did not know before reading the article?

3. What was the cumulative impact of the article on your views?

# Article 17

## PRO-CHOICERS AND THE 'NOT A PERSON' ARGUMENT

**Gist**: a radical challenge to a major pro-choice argument

The notion that that which results from the fusion of a man's sperm cell and a woman's ovum, called a zygote up to 12 weeks in development, is not a person seems, on the surface, to be a compelling argument for abortion. But appearances can be deceptive and this argument is no better than a red herring or smaller fish because it is biologically erroneous and very defective legally.

From an elementary genus and species standpoint the argument is on life support. The offspring of a particular genus and species cannot but be in essence like the genus and species from which it springs! If a human couple engages in unprotected sex and fertilisation culminates in conception then another human has been conceived.

It is indisputable, scientifically, that life begins at conception. A human life begins and that one-celled zygote is a stage in human development through which we have all passed (just as we have all passed through the foetus, embryo, infancy, adolescent stages of human development). Critical note: we did not emerge eventually from these stages in development, but biologically we were all once a human zygote, a human foetus, a human embryo, a human infant, a human adolescent and so on towards adulthood.

At every stage we are all humans, just different in size/shape maybe, but humans nonetheless. That's basic biology!

At no stage of our development would any sensible person think that we were canine or feline or whatever genus/species kind other than human.

I am no lawyer, but from my reading of legal literature, lawyers need to probe more deeply the logical link made by the US Supreme Court between proof of the beginning of life and personhood in Roe v. Wade.

To me, a non-lawyer, the Court blundered somewhat in that it had reputable scientific evidence available to it that life begins at conception. Two 1968 text book quotations should suffice.

1. *Human Embryology* (3rd edition) by Bradley Patten says at p.43:

> It is the penetration of the ovum by a spermatozoan and the resultant mingling of the nuclear material each brings to the union that constitutes the culmination of the process of fertilization and **marks the initiation of the life of a new individual**. [emphasis added]

2. Dr. Louis Fridhanler, in the medical textbook *Biology of Gestation* (vol. 1) edited by N.S. Assau, calls fertilization: "that wondrous moment that marks **the beginning of life for a new unique individual.**" [p. 76 emphasis added]

Yet listen to Justice Blackmun, speaking for the Court in 1973: "We need not resolve the difficult question of when life begins…"

Additionally, on the legal front, as I pointed out in my *Jamaica Observer* letter 'Legal Puzzles concerning Pregnant Women' (March 19, 2019), there are legal conventions that attribute personhood to the unborn from conception. Even if one indulges the nicety of legal personhood as opposed to personhood in fact, there is much to ponder from quasi legal and other legal traditions that speak to the personhood of the unborn.

As Lawyer/Philosopher/Theologian Prof. John Warwick Montgomery points out:

> ...in the area of property law Anglo-American jurisprudence has maintained remarkable concern for fetal rights...In that realm of the common law—property rights—where the protections afforded are the most unqualified and absolute (in rem), the fetus has most consistently been given recognition from the moment of conception... (In his *Slaughter of the Innocents*, 116)

Montgomery goes on to say that the International and Comparative Law of Human Rights favours the unborn and so too does the non-obligatory Declaration of the Rights of the Child which states in its preamble that the child "requires juridical protection before as well as after birth." (118) On the same page Montgomery adds that "the American Convention of Human Rights, which entered into force in 1978, declares (Article 4) that "Every person has the right to have his life respected. This right

## SOCIETAL CONCERNS

shall be protected by law, and, in general, from the moment of conception..."

Raising the issue of personhood concerning a human offspring at any stage of development, given the available biological and legal material, must be seen for what it really is, a smelly red herring and a desperate clutching at a barely visible straw.

Observer 9/4/19

# DISCUSSION QUESTIONS

1. In what way did the author appeal to your mind as opposed to your emotions?

2. What did you learn that you did not know before reading the article?

3. How, if at all, have your views on abortion been affected by the article?

# Article 18

## THE BIBLE AND INDICTABLE IGNORANCE

**Gist**: The author chides his friend and Bible critic Dr. Michael Abrahams

So, my friend Dr. Michael Abrahams regards the Bible as a dangerous book. Well, well.

When I was a young Christian growing up in Montego Bay there was a very popular song about Jesus which encouraged Christians to seek to make people know about Him. The song was 'Everybody ought to know.' It was sometimes sung in a quasi-call and response fashion with the thrice repeated call "everybody ought to know" and the *sotto voce* (subdued voice) response each time being "some

## SOCIETAL CONCERNS

people don't know." Then came 'everybody ought to know who Jesus is.'

Every natural scientist (like Michael) **ought to know** that modern science's experimental tap roots owe a debt to the Bible's notion of a carefully crafted orderly universe (Gen. 1).

I go further. Modern science not only had its experimental tap roots in the biblical worldview of a purposive, orderly, created world, but as careful historians of science ought to know, virtually all scientists from the Middle Ages to the mid-eighteenth century—many of whom were seminal thinkers—not only were sincere Christians but were often inspired by biblical postulates and premises in their theories that sought to explain and predict natural phenomena.

The names include Leonardo da Vinci (1452-1519) in human physiology; Gregor Mendel (1822-1884) in genetics; Nicolaus Copernicus (1475-1543), Johannes Kepler (1571-1630) and Galileo Galilei (1564-1642) in astronomy. In physics: Isaac Newton (1642-1727), Gottfried Leibniz (1646-1716), Blaise Pascal (1623-1662), Georg Simon Ohm (1787-1854), André Ampere (1775-1836) and Michael Faraday (1791-1867). In chemistry: Robert Boyle (1627-1691), Antoine Lavoisier (1743-1794), George Washington Carver (c.1864-1943) and in medicine, Louis Pasteur (1822-1895) and Joseph Lister (1827-1912).

## A CONTROVERSIAL CLERGYMAN

Not to know this is indictable ignorance.

The most abiding alternative to the biblical doctrine of a universe created in time by God has been the scientific notion that the universe is eternal, has no beginning and therefore needs no beginner.

In 1913, astronomer Vesto Slipher discovered that a dozen galaxies near earth were moving away from the earth at very high speeds, ranging up to 2 million miles per hour. This discovery led to the realization that the Universe was expanding which also meant that the Universe had a beginning.

The reaction to Slipher's discovery and the implications of that discovery for the origin of the Universe provoked some odd reactions from scientists.

Albert Einstein in a letter to one of his colleagues said, "This circumstance [of an expanding Universe] irritates me."

Arthur Eddington, in 1931 said, "...the notion of a beginning is repugnant to me...the expanding Universe is preposterous...incredible...it leaves me cold."

Allan Sandage, another astronomer, said concerning the evidence that the Universe had a beginning, "It is such a strange conclusion...it cannot really be true."

## SOCIETAL CONCERNS

The Cosmic Background Explorer satellite, in 1992, provided additional confirming information on the nature of the origin of the Universe. The findings of the satellite attracted the attention of major newspapers and TV programmes across the world.

George Smoot, project leader for the Cosmic Background Explorer satellite declared, "What we have found is evidence for the birth of the Universe...It's like looking at God."

Mikey, my esteemed friend, not to know these things is indictable ignorance and this is only in your field of the natural sciences.

If I was a contracted columnist (assured of being published) I could go on to detail the Bible's influence on many things that western civilization prizes like the value of humankind and of life, sexual morality, charity and compassion, law and the arts.

Everybody ought to know these things but some people don't know because of indictable ignorance!!

Rispeck mi bredrin.

Gleaner 10/7/17

## QUESTIONS FOR DISCUSSION

1. How is this article a defence of the non-dangerous nature of the Bible?

2. What might you conclude about the Bible from the article?

3. What might you read 'between the lines' of the author's charge of indictable ignorance?

# Part III

# LEGAL AFFAIRS

# Article 19

## JUDICIAL COURAGE: RULING VS. REASONING

**Gist**: The opening paragraph says it all

The Buggery Law may need to be declared unconstitutional but not on the basis of the shoddy arguments advanced in the *Gleaner* editorial of November 29, 2018 ('Judicial Courage and the Buggery Law').

This editorial prompted some issues that demand clearer thinking:

1) An acute distinction needs to be made between a judicial ruling and the reasoning behind that

ruling, similar to a conclusion and the supporting arguments toward that conclusion.

2) The *Gleaner's* lawyers should have been consulted, or they should have proofread the editorial better before it was printed to avoid what I, as a non-lawyer, saw as ignorance about how legal jurisdictions operate.

3) We all need to bury the inane criticism of a law based simply on its age. Whether the law was passed in 1864 or 1800 BC (cf. murder in the code of Hammurabi) is tangential to the content and probative value of the law!

I sent the *Gleaner* the first of a 2-part logical critique of the Orozco ruling from Belize but it was not published. This is the *Gleaner's* right so to do, since I am not a contracted columnist. It would help though to find out how many lawyers have actually read the whole judgement and that, analytically, beyond skimming for the final ruling/verdict.

I have been reliably informed that neither the Belize nor the Trinidad and Tobago Court's ruling, even on a similar case, has any binding legal force on our highest Court here though either ruling may be regarded as persuasive.

I make bold to say if our highest court finds the argumentation in the Orozco ruling even persuasive,

## A CONTROVERSIAL CLERGYMAN

I would be very deeply disappointed in it, intellectually.

I found aspects of the Orozco ruling puzzling, both legally and especially logically, and I apologize for saying that the reasoning on a key point of law, namely 'public morality' as per the constitution of Belize, reminded me of an idiotic statute that was on the books in Kansas, USA, for years before the idiocy was spotted and the statute repealed.

That Kansas statute said: "When two trains approach each other at a [railroad] crossing, they both shall come to a full stop and neither shall start up until the other has clean gone."

Chief Justice Benjamin of Belize said:

> [69] The sole limitation relied upon by the Defendant is that of public morality. In paragraph 8 of the Ramjeet affidavit, section 9 (2) is cited.
>
> Section 9(2) reads in part,
>
> 9 (2). Nothing contained in or done under the authority of any law shall be held to be inconsistent with or in contravention of this section to the extent that the law in question makes reasonable provision

(a) that is required in the interests of defence, public safety, public order, public morality, public health...

Some Church leaders, allowed as interested parties, raised the public morality issue and the eminent Chief Justice ruled,

> [81] There can be no doubt that the Reverend gentlemen deposed to views that they sincerely and conscientiously hold, and that are representative of the majority of the Christian community and perhaps of the population of Belize. However, from the perspective of legal principle, the Court cannot act upon prevailing majority views or what is popularly accepted as moral. The evidence may be supportive, but this does not satisfy the justification of public morality. There must be demonstrated that some harm will be caused should the proscribed conduct be rendered unregulated. No evidence has been presented as to the real likelihood of such harm.

So, the learned jurist concedes that the views expressed by the clergymen "are representative of the majority of the Christian community and perhaps of the population of Belize," but says this

## A CONTROVERSIAL CLERGYMAN

"does not satisfy the justification of public morality." I ask in amazed ignorance, why not?

On what basis should/could a Court determine public morality beyond assessing public sentiment about particular moral issues?

According to the eminent CJ, one would have to establish by evidence that "some harm will be caused should the proscribed conduct be rendered unregulated." But "[N]o evidence has been presented as to the real likelihood of such harm."

Notice a few odd things here. The possible views of the population of Belize does not, without more, qualify as 'public morality'! Then the Chief Justice, in my unlearned view, indulges a muddled logical stretch about the need for harm. By what legal, linguistic or philosophical canon? Public morality does not require a concept of [certain or likely] harm to qualify as public morality.

The CJ seems unaware that the construction "will be caused" is one of certainty and is not equal in force to the construction "real likelihood of such harm." This latter construction suggests a lower degree of proof along the descending spectrum, certain, likely, probable, possible.

No one can prove with certainty the consequences of most acts but some can be argued for beyond reasonable doubt (= probable or likely), but why is the harm component even invoked by the CJ?

The section of the judge's ruling dealing with the claimant's violated right to dignity was also very, very suspect in reasoning.

The learned CJ delivered himself thus:

> [65] The Claimant submitted that section 53 of the Criminal Code is in breach of his fundamental right to recognition of his human dignity by:
>
> (i) stigmatising him as being a criminal by virtue of being a homosexual...

How does a law stigmatize any person "as being a criminal" even if one is engaged in unlawful conduct, unless that person is convicted of such offence in court? Based on this sloppy line of reasoning everybody could claim to be stigmatized "as being a criminal" simply by the existence of laws that proscribe certain behaviours **without ever having been arrested and convicted in court for said breach of the law.**

The CJ relied on a constitutional challenge to South Africa's common law prohibition on sodomy *vis-à-vis* dignity and cited a dictum from Ackerman J which says in part:

"Its symbolic effect is to state that in the eyes of our legal system all gay men are criminals. The stigma thus attached to a significant proportion of our population is manifest. But the harm imposed by the criminal law is far more than symbolic. As a result of the criminal offence, gay men are at risk of arrest, prosecution and conviction of the offence of sodomy simply because they seek to engage in sexual conduct which is part of their experience of being human..."

I know too little about how legal reasoning works, it seems, to be able to appreciate how these two eminent jurists can regard a legal prohibition as rendering a person as a criminal minus arrest, prosecution and conviction.

It gets worse on my jaundiced analysis in that the quoted dictum from Ackerman J continues to say:

"There can be no doubt that the existence of a law which punishes a form of sexual expression for gay men degrades and devalues gay men in our broader society. As such it is a palpable invasion of their dignity and a breach of section 10 of our Constitution ..."

Say what, Justice Ackerman?! How then doesn't every penalty in law degrade and devalue people in general, thus invading their dignity in breach of the South African constitution?!

## LEGAL AFFAIRS

CJ Benjamin immediately after reliance on Ackerman drops this howler:

"The foregoing dictum is in all respects applicable to the plight of the Claimant based on the averments in his 1st affidavit. He is entitled to pray in his aid, section 3(c) of the Constitution and assert a violation of his right to human dignity as a person."

You have got to be kidding me! This unclear even illogical dictum is now to ground a claimed violation of a right to human dignity?

Critical thinking, aka logical reasoning, is necessary not only for Primary Exit Profile (PEP) students but for all of us, eminent jurists included.

*Gleaner* 23/12/18

# DISCUSSION QUESTIONS

1. Locate and read the *Gleaner* editorial; then advance your reasons for siding logically with the *Gleaner* or with the author.

2. Were you clear on the issues dealt with, and if not why not?

3. If the author had read this in a Court of law could he be cited for contempt, and for what specifically?

# Article 20

## LAW AND ETHICS: NATURAL OR UNNATURAL BEDFELLOWS?

**Gist**: Probing the relationship between law and ethics

Prompted by the protracted debate about the buggery law, gruesome murders, abortion, corruption, the ganja industry, etc., I wish to highlight a dilemma that all free societies face, namely, deciding on the relationship between positive law and ethics. What is positive law and what do we mean by ethics?

"Ethics, or moral philosophy...is the systematic endeavor to understand moral concepts and justify moral principles and theories. It undertakes to analyze such concepts as 'right,' 'wrong,'

## LEGAL AFFAIRS

'permissible,' 'ought,' 'good,' and 'evil,' in their moral contexts." (Louis Pojman, *Ethical Theory: Classic and Contemporary Readings*, 2002, p.1)

"The term positive law refers to laws made by man that require some specific action. These are statutes, codes, and regulations that have been enacted by a legislature. By contrast, 'natural law' refers to principles that are universal in society, governing moral acts." (online dictionary)

The wording on the front of a tee-shirt I got after a recent presentation in Antigua sums up the issue somewhat: "What's legal isn't always right".

It is not every positive law that neatly overlaps with ethics, but ponder some instructive comments from lawyers and a wannabe lawyer about the inevitable overlaps and see how cogent their ideas are.

The first is from a wannabe whose name I withhold to protect the person's innocence.

"Positive law in any society enshrines or at least reflects somewhat that society's ethico-moral outlook or highest aspirations. Statutes are therefore moral censors."

Whether the statute commands tax-paying (at risk of a penalty) or prohibits extortion (again at risk of a penalty), implied in both command and prohibition, is a value system, a suggested 'oughtness' about certain behaviours.

Now to real lawyers.

"...since all law necessarily reflects a moral value system of some kind, there is every reason to have it reflect the proper...value system." (John Warwick Montgomery, *Human Rights & Human Dignity*, 2019, p. 180)

The million-dollar challenge is determining the "proper value system!"

Interact now with a statement from Roman Stoic lawyer Cicero (106-43 BC):

> I find it has been the opinion of the wisest men that Law is not a product of human thought, nor is it any enactment of peoples, but something eternal which rules the whole universe by its wisdom in command and prohibition. Thus, they have been accustomed to say that Law is the primal and ultimate mind of God. (*De legibus*, bk. 2, chap. 4)

Though we can outline different basic ethical systems our problem is not thereby solved. Montgomery again:

"The problem of establishing sound ethical standards in the legal profession and the wider

## LEGAL AFFAIRS

problem of which this is but one aspect—that of finding ethical norms for the evaluation of positive law in general—becomes immensely more acute when we see total societies operating with legal and ethical values directly opposed to our own." (reference regrettably lost)

The fundamental problem during the international Nuremburg trials of so-called 'crimes against humanity' committed by Nazi military officials after the holocaust was, deciding by whose legal standard the men would be tried. Their simple yet profound retort was "we were simply following orders."

The chief prosecutor wrestled with the ethico-legal norm of not taking human life without legal justification but faced, also, the military 'ought' of the Nazis on trial "obey the order then question later."

Though it irks our sensibilities, 'obey the order then question or challenge it later' makes sense in security services because free thought could endanger the lives of fellow security colleagues in a crisis situation. The prosecutor said, I gather: "So what we need is a law above the laws." Cicero resurrected?

Reflect further on the dilemma in the lament of the late Arthur Leff, Professor of Law at Duke

University. In his 1979 lecture "Unspeakable Ethics, Unnatural Law," he said:

> I want to believe—and so do you—in a complete, transcendent and immanent set of propositions about right and wrong, findable rules that authoritatively and unambiguously direct us how to live righteously. I also want to believe—and so do you—in no such thing, but rather that we are wholly free, not only to choose for ourselves what we ought to do, but to decide for ourselves, individually and as a species, what we ought to be. What we want, Heaven help us, **is simultaneously to be perfectly ruled and perfectly free, that is, at the same time to discover the right and the good and to create it**." ("Unspeakable Ethics, Unnatural Law," *Duke Law Journal* 6 (December 1979): 1229, my emphasis)

No society can escape the challenge I am raising here. Law and Ethics are in fact bedfellows; we can only quibble about whether, or to what degree, they are naturally or unnaturally so.

By the way, though our democratic traditions suggest that we have referenda on some controversial issues, or that MPs should consult their constituencies on some such issues (like abortion or the buggery law), the result of these exercises fare no better, in essence, than what happens in most churches that ask members 'what do you think the Bible passage means?'

In essence this may just be, and often is, pooling ignorance!

Observer, 14/11/18

## DISCUSSION QUESTIONS

1. How would you evaluate the author's view about the interplay between law and ethics?

2. Develop an informational presentation on 'legal ethics' or 'ethics in the legal profession.'

3. Why is the popular view that an 'honest lawyer is an oxymoron' a species of slander?

# Article 21

## MICHAEL, BE FAIR TO GOD

**Gist**: Countering a Bible critic's claim about God in the Old Testament

My esteemed friend Dr. Michael Abrahams in his column elsewhere in the press (*Gleaner*, September 7, 2015) contends that God in the Old Testament is not merciful. I am countering with some philosophical and legal pointers.

If being merciful is not meting out the [just] punishment deserved by a guilty offender, then a plea for or expectation of mercy is, in essence, seeking a 'bly,' (a Jamaicanism for unmerited even undeserved favour).

# LEGAL AFFAIRS

Though it is a widespread view that a 'good' person would/should be more than fair in dealing with others, one needs to question the basis of such a view. Why so?

So, I ask my friend Michael, why should God be more merciful than just (i.e. meting out commensurate deserts to law-breakers)?

Let it be known that 'mercy' is not inherent in our judicial system. The prerogative of mercy resides with our [titular] monarch and thus with our Governor General. A plea for mercy is really begging for something beyond strict justice (hence extra judicial). There is no right here at all. If one disagrees with punishment, per se, or a degree of punishment, then the germane issue is not mercy but a legal challenge of some kind.

Imagine an accused charging that our Supreme Court, the Court of Appeal and as well the Privy Council are more concerned with being just than with being merciful. Such a charge, levelled at the highest legal tribunals in our judicial system, would be, at best, laughable, and at worst, totally misguided.

As I urged in a recent public forum "Is the God of the Old Testament a Moral Monster?" borrowing the words of H.E. Guillebaud, "The distorted picture of God as a mildly benevolent Heavenly Father whose patience is inexhaustible, who will never deal more hardly with his creatures than the most easy-going of earthly parents...is a complete misrepresentation of the God of the Bible." (In his *Some Moral Difficul— ties of the Bible*, 1941, 110).

I went on to say, Anyone, (whether a Christian or a non-theistic critic) who registers internally or expresses publicly a problem with the sanctions on human misbehaviour recorded in the Old Testament, whether directly or indirectly attributed to God, needs to justify that position.

The objector may have problems at best with the degrees of punishment threatened or administered in the Old Testament or at worst with the notion of punishment itself especially coming from a loving/merciful God.

A summary challenge to both positions would be to ask if the said objector has a similar problem with sanctions threatened or administered in modern law or with the notion of punishment in law. Indeed, any objector who says yes to both positions must, if logically consistent, have a problem with laws and the concomitant sanctions in law, since laws without sanctions are like dogs without teeth and so unable to bite or virtually useless.

As lawyer/philosopher/theologian Prof. John Warwick Montgomery advises:

# LEGAL AFFAIRS

All law — whether physical law or societal law — involves two elements: order and compulsion [i.e. sanctions]...Scientific laws describe regularities in the physical universe. They also — and inevitably— entail sanctions, that is to say, negative consequences if we disregard or violate them...Finally we come to the law of the land — juridical law.

This is the law that is enforced not by social ostracism (as is custom) or by moral opprobrium (as is the moral law), but by state sanctions. Most modern nations have legal systems that distinguish civil law and criminal law.

Civil law attaches penalties...to acts which cause quantifiable or objectively provable harm to others. Criminal law deals with those far more serious acts which are inherently harmful to the society as a whole (homicide, physical attacks, stealing, corruption, etc.), and attaches much more serious penalties to their commission (incarceration and sometimes even the death penalty). (In his *Christ As Centre and Circumference*, 2012, 572-573.)

It may seem politically correct to move away from notions of retributive justice to restorative justice, but practically and philosophically are we rubbishing the notion of 'commensurate desserts,' the jugular vein of justice in law? This is a very thorny issue in modern jurisprudence, which is the philosophy of law.

If the objector simply has a problem with the degrees of punishment threatened or meted out, then such an objection implies knowledge of a yardstick beyond God's pronouncement that renders the sanctions in Scripture as unjust or excessive. This also presupposes that the objector has intimate knowledge of how God sees particular sins or offences and has knowledge superior to God's re commensurate desserts.

There is yet another matter for the objector to deal with re God and our legal system. If one is not opposed to all sanctions in our legal system why deny the Sovereign God/Judge of the Universe a right that is allowed to human law courts —the right to punish wrongdoing?

Finally, a thin slice of Divine mercy in the Old Testament. The flood was not terminal, one family was spared to give rise to another population of humans. The Canaanite people group, the Amorites, got a mercy period of approximately 430 years before judgement (Gen. 15:16); Sodom and Gomorrah were punished only after God could not find ten righteous persons therein (Gen. 18:32); Jonah's problem with his call to prophesy conditional doom upon Nineveh was that he

## LEGAL AFFAIRS

disagreed with God's willingness to forgive and not punish a repentant nation.

The Old Testament refrain that "the Lord is longsuffering, and of great mercy..." or similar sentiments (Num. 14:18; 1Chron. 16:34 and several Psalms) emerge from the writers' familiarity with this attribute of God.

Let's read carefully, analyze properly and as weird as it sounds, be fair to God.

Gleaner 7/9/15

## DISCUSSION QUESTIONS

1. What is your evaluation of the logical flow of the author's argumentation? (provide evidence from the article)

2. Identify and comment concisely on any logical fallacy that you detected in the article.

3. If you were Dr. Abrahams how would you respond to the article?

# Article 22

## CHUCK CHALLENGING CHURCH'S OLD TEACHINGS

**Gist**: Chiding Justice Minister Chuck

I have read that our Justice Minister, Delroy Chuck, has suggested that parliamentarians should tackle the Church about its adherence to centuries old moral teaching from the Bible, but I refuse to believe the report.

No lawyer of Mr. Chuck's eminence could advance such a silly age-based argument!

I know that many reject the Bible out of hand because it is too old a document to be appealed to in the modern age.

How does the age of a document necessarily negate the wisdom or value of the document's content? What would such critics say about the almost universal millennia-old taboo on murder, adultery and stealing in every culture studied in antiquity and the abiding negative sentiments and even legal sanctions (excepting for adultery) on those practices today?

Should we by this age-based reasoning trash all literature from antiquity, including the revered pieces of Egyptian literature for some critics and the equally revered pieces of Greek or Roman literature for other critics?

A comparative survey of Ancient Near Eastern law codes is quite instructive: the old Hittite laws of 1650-1500 BC; the 1800 BC Babylonian code of Hammurabi or the oldest Egyptian laws all have some taboos that have modern legal descendants of a kind.

The terribly misunderstood biblical legal principle of the *Lex talionis,* 'an eye for an eye...' (c. 1500 BC) is, in modern jurisprudence, a valuable legal principle = the punishment should fit the crime, so if I tailgate you and damage the rear bumper of your Honda Fit don't try to make a claim for a BMW X7!! The claimed whatever must be comparable to the damaged whatever.

Indeed, the Bible's millennia-old aversion to homosexual practices may have a more plausible explanation. As Robert Gagnon says, "...the antiquity and durability of a given prohibition against immoral conduct often indicates its workability, effectiveness, and elasticity as a cultural model rather than its contemporary irrelevance." (*The Bible & Homosexual Practice*, 29)

If the report I read accurately reflects the sentiments of our Minister of Justice, then Mr. Chuck needs to come up with a more sensible basis for a 'social revolution' against the Church. As the French would say *mettez vous en garde, mon frere!!*

*Gleaner's* letter of the day (abridged and recaptioned) 12/6/17)

## DISCUSSION QUESTIONS

1. What logical merit would you apply to the article and why?

2. Since we are in changing times why should we not move away from very old taboos?

3. Why (implied by Chuck's challenge) is a new law necessarily superior to an old one?

# Part IV

# CHURCH MATTERS

# Article 23

## UNDERSTANDING AND DEALING WITH CLERGY SEXUAL ABUSE

"If you have never felt a strong pull to sexual intercourse, you are abnormal, too old, too young, or 'too lie' (i.e. untruthful)." (Chisholm: *Plain Talk on Sex CD*)

**Gist:** Addressing a current scandal

Late last year (2018) Maverley Gospel Hall invited me to do a session on the topic of this article. Very early in the session I strengthened my CD opener and substituted sexual immorality for sexual intercourse. Below is an edited version of what I shared.

## CHURCH MATTERS

Understanding (making sense of...)

Registering a desire for sexual intercourse as a Christian is not evidence that you are either 'old man' or no longer 'new man', but that you are simply human.

The Church, in far too many places, has been too shy in dealing with sexual issues up front in worship gatherings. Yes, I mean in Sabbath and Sunday morning services, not just in midweek or special meetings when so few are in attendance.

The pervasive reality of a feeling for sexual intercourse itself opens the possibility/reality of struggles with sexual immorality which means that the Church cannot avoid teaching on sex and sexuality because sexual desires affect everybody, Church members as well as those who need to be in the Church.

Let us quickly clarify the term sexuality. For me (I'm no Psychologist) there are three things involved in the concept of sexuality: sexual identity, gender identity and sexual orientation.

Sexual identity relates to one's genetic makeup, the particular combination of X and Y chromosomes. The genes of our being and hormones (the relative presence or absence of them) determine how masculine or feminine we appear physically and influence the intensity of our sexual desire.

## A CONTROVERSIAL CLERGYMAN

Gender identity relates to the inner sense or picture we have of ourselves as male or female and is largely determined by social and psychological forces. Gender identity is formed usually during infancy and childhood.

There is also the reality that some persons are described as 'gender non-conforming'. These persons don't accept the traditional binary (2-form) gender-typing based on physiology and so we have the LGBT community (i.e., the community of Lesbians, Gay, Bisexual and Trans-gender persons) and at times one may read or hear about the LGBTQ or LGBTI or even LGBTA grouping where the Q (=questioning) or I (=intersex) or the A (=Asexual) are species or subsets of Trans-gender).

So then to put this in the form of an equation, Sexuality = sexual identity + gender identity + sexual orientation. Put differently, and less precisely, your sexuality involves who you are sexually, who you feel like sexually and who/what you feel for sexually.

It should help as well to look at the most popular sexual orientations. [I then looked at the 5 basic ones: heterosexuality, homosexuality, bisexuality, bestiality and asexuality]

Let me say some more here because some Church folk are too conservative and 'spiritual' to face the issues squarely.

## CHURCH MATTERS

We must be clear in our minds that God made us as psycho-sexual creatures. So, in the perfection of Eden, Adam and Eve came from the hand of God with sex organs and with erogenous zones and with the capacity to desire and feel for sexual intercourse.

So sexual intercourse was not created after humankind sinned but was a God-given and delightful reality before 'the fall' (the first sin of our foreparents Adam and Eve). The Devil had nothing to do with the origin of sexual intercourse. Only God could have created something so sweet! Okay, track me down and wash out my mouth with industrial strength Jeyes!

If anyone here is in doubt about it, just take it by faith from me. Church members are struggling more with sexual issues than with the major doctrines of the faith. Church leaders need to scratch where members are itching!

There is only one kind of sex act that is countenanced in Scripture, that is a married man with his wife; all other sex acts are expressly forbidden in the Word.

But, know as well, that the laws of our country forbid certain sex acts. So, with reference to sexual intercourse we have the moral dimension and the legal dimension, and these are separate domains.

# A CONTROVERSIAL CLERGYMAN

So, the peculiar Jamaican legal definition of sexual intercourse is penile/vaginal, with all other romantic/erotic acts seen as sexual intimacy (involving mouth, anus, between breasts, etc.) but not qualifying as sexual intercourse.

Our law forbids sexual intercourse involving persons under 16 years of age. This means that whether you are a boy or a girl you cannot legally consent/agree to sexual intercourse. Regardless of how your body looks or how 'horny' you feel, it is unlawful for anyone to have sexual intercourse with you, whether your sex partner is someone of your age/gender or a 'greyback' big man or sexy big woman.

So, whoever you are, having sexual intercourse with someone below the age of consent (16) is at once immoral and criminal!

What though is 'sexual abuse?' I would begin by saying it is 'beyond the approved behavioural boundaries and is double-edged (illegal/immoral).' Generally, going beyond the boundaries of the moral or the legal is abuse, and a most basic component of this is doing without defensible consent or trying to offer what is not wanted by another, which is a species of harassment.

So then, clergy sexual abuse is sexual behaviour from a clergy person which is immoral and/or illegal or inappropriate. I add inappropriate to immoral and illegal because some species of sexual abuse may not strictly speaking qualify as outright immoral or illegal but still not fitting/expedient/appropriate coming from a Christian or a clergy person.

For example, sexually suggestive talk (including sexting, rude jokes, touching/fondling, sexual grooming). Grooming is a process by which someone befriends and gains the trust of a child (and sometimes the child's friends and family) in order to take advantage of the child for sexual purposes. Discernment is necessary here, Parents.

There has to be some degree of pathology (illness) when a big man finds himself fascinated with thinking/dreaming about and seeking opportunities to have sexual intercourse with a minor, 'a likkle pickney.' Such a man would need, in addition to prayer/fasting, serious psycho-therapeutic help.

(Psychologist Dr. Joan Pinkney was in the congregation so I asked her to say a few words here).

A person's sexual fantasy is something to take seriously re getting help. A sexual fantasy is an unfulfilled or a hoped-for/hope-to–be-repeated sexual desire/wish. Fantasies are thus time-bombs waiting to explode, hopefully in the right context.

# A CONTROVERSIAL CLERGYMAN

Fantasy has the ability to drive the male as a slave-master would a slave. The role of fantasy in the mature male is critical to understanding his fears, frustrations, and especially his sexual compulsions.

For good reason Jesus advised caution on lust – fantasy/mental sex. Lust is a major problem for most men. The man who claims never to have had a struggle with lust needs to be reminded that lying is a sin that can end you up in the lake of fire (Rev. 21:8). (For a developed treatment of lust vs. admiration see my CD *Plain Talk on Sex*).

A baseline test of the distinction between lust and admiration is, for me, the 'penis test'. It is possible, though rare, for a man to sustain an erection while simply admiring, and it is just barely possible, though highly unlikely, that a man without Erectile Dysfunction could be lusting without an erection.

In admiration, the woman's form and features (curves and contours) are seen as attractive/beautiful ends in themselves and God or Nature is credited with skill. In lust those same curves and contours are desired as pleasurable means to a man's sexual ends. God/Nature is not in the picture, the one lusting simply wants to romp with the creation.

That's my approach to understanding the problem, and here are a few pointers for dealing with it:

*1. Honest self-awareness is necessary.*

So, if you find yourself admiring minors (boys and/or girls) and every now and then you even have an erection while admiring any of them, you need clinical help!

May I throw in a statement here for us all to ponder? The frequency with which a [married] person lusts is an index of his/her I.Q., not Intelligence Quotient but Infidelity Quotient.

Never assume you are stronger than you really are. I said, in a sermon in Florida where our daughter and her husband were present, that I have not committed the sins of other men, not because I lack their strong desire for immorality, but maybe I just lack their opportunity. But if opportunity met desire, I would be dead meat like anybody else! My daughter said after the sermon, "Papi, that was the most honest and boldest sermon I have heard in a long while."

Friends, I struggle too (and I thank God for friends like Drs. Barry Davidson, Joan Pinkney and Neal Walker especially, from whom I can get loving but firm guidance). But I try to be as honest as I can with myself, and readily ask very close friends to pray for/with me whenever I sense a weakening in resolve re purity. Seriously, one of my favourite hymns of reality therapy is 'Prone to wander, Lord, I feel it...'

2. Depth psychotherapeutic assessment of potential clergy candidates and periodic similar assessment while serving **should be mandatory.**

As Dr. Pinkney urges:

> A course in Human sexuality and therapy sessions should form part of any training for clergy to unearth sexual fantasies, effects of childhood sexual/other types of abuse, self-esteem/self-concept/esteem issues, sexual orientation issues (in keeping with Biblical principles), dealing with suppressed sexual energy (in keeping with the call to celibacy/purity and pastoral ministry), exercising self-control etc.

3. Redemptive therapeutic options for those who are in need via disclosure or diagnosis/detection/discernment

Dr. Pinkney once again:

Once sexual abuse is made public, restoration to public service may be difficult in our culture for the offender, as the laity and society may not see them capable to carry out the Lord's work. The offence carries a stigma which may be the closest one gets to the unpardonable sin (by humans). Our culture does not tolerate homosexuality at any level – therein lies another challenge. However, systems should be in place in the church for redemption and restoration. This must be ongoing and handled by appropriately trained personnel in the field of counseling/ psychology/psychiatry.

But bearing in mind the separate domains of the immoral and the illegal, clergy who sexually abuse minors ought to be reported to the Police and not simply left untouched or moved to another church/parish/circuit. Church folk may forgive the [repentant] fallen (on the moral plane) but dare not assume authority within the legal plane.

This is tough love to protect both the victim(s), potential victims and the guilty. Sexual proclivities of whatever kind are almost addictive so a repeated sexual abuse is not just possible but probable, even likely.

4. *Effective accountability systems/partners should be required in all denominations and independent churches.*

These would need the input of highly trained therapists including Christian sexologists. Clinical Psychologist, Dr. the Rev. Neal Walker, my Jamaica Theological Seminary batch mate, says:

> In general, we don't have an effective system in place to evaluate our clergy. We go to Bible college or seminary. We graduate with honours, with advanced degrees. We are thrown into the pastorate or into other leadership positions. We may hold denominational conventions and conferences but very, very few of us ever completed a course (one course) in Gender and Sexuality. But even worse, very few ministers receive any kind of treatment or one-on-one session with a trained professional therapist. Very few!

He continues:

> I have argued in presentations that pastoring (legitimate pastoring) is the hardest job on earth. Forget the 30 mega churches we know about ... the run-of-the-mill pastor is a sufferer. He (or she) has few friends, hardly shares his/her heart, struggles to avoid cussing out people who call

themselves elders and deacons (and I mean using the F bomb), receives no good pay and fewer thank yous, struggles with porn, hides any sins committed and acts like he/she is enjoying pastoring. I deal daily with the dark side of human life, but my 20 years of pastoring were the most challenging years of my life.

Every clergy should avail himself/herself (men in particular) to one solid full year of couch sessions. I did and am happy my clinical program demanded it. If we cannot afford to seek professional services, find a seasoned person who could hear you out. We (clergy) all need a safe harbor where we could unpack ourselves.

Friends, I leave it there and open now for your questions and comments.

Observer 4/8/19, Gleaner (in 2 parts) 4/8/19 and 11/8/19

## DISCUSSION QUESTIONS

1. Imagine yourself in the congregation, what comment or question would you have raised with the author?

## A CONTROVERSIAL CLERGYMAN

2. What, if anything, in the article shocked or surprised you, and why?

3. What impact, if any, do you think this article would have on clergy persons and others who are inclined to abusing minors, and why, either way?

# Article 24

## CRITICAL THINKING AND THE CHURCH

**Gist**: Blunt advice on the topic

Nonsense or sloppy reasoning is not sanctified because it happens in church. It is still deserving of criticism and correction.

Pastors and lay preachers need to be committed to modelling from the pulpit and cultivating in the pew at-easeness with and love for critical thinking. After all thinking deeply and well is encouraged in texts like Isaiah 1:3 and 18; Acts 17:2 and Christians ought to love God progressively with all their mind!

If feedback and guided interaction are necessary in the teaching-learning process then these ought to be utilised in Christian education. A few suggestions may prove useful.

Since the early 1990s while serving at Phillippo Baptist Church in Spanish Town I began experimenting with what I called then 'afterglow.' Basically, I told the congregation that I am open for their questions after each sermon and I reserve the right to call on anyone to answer questions about the main points of the sermon/study. At first, folk did not like the idea because for some "it's an intrusion in worship," but after a while they recognised the value of the exercise for learning. I still do that as a guest preacher here and abroad and find that the youth and young adults especially welcome it.

I know that in certain quarters this idea would not even be prayed about but that is because the tradition that "Pastor is God's representative" is taken to mean Pastor is always clear in mind and sensible in argumentation. But even in such quarters, folk know that this is not true.

The obsession with "saying nothing noisily and stylishly" is far too popular with pulpit and pew alike. I told a good friend of a Pentecostal persuasion that her church is guilty of a species of blasphemy, always associating God with what is "loud, late and long!"

God can speak through a 'still small voice' and Christians need to value punctuality and brevity/conciseness in oral presentations.

Why the shouting from the pulpit? The microphone already amplifies your natural voice. Don't ask me to tell my neighbour, or repeat an inanity after you, or give you an amen for some trite or unclear notion you just spouted! Not happening, but then maybe I just need Jesus!

If the sermon/talk is constructed as well as any speech should be, there are main points and subpoints to aid memory, all in a logical flow bookended by an arresting opener/introduction and a purposeful conclusion. Planned feedback forces better sermon preparation re content and structure.

Another aid to critical thinking in the pew is case-study discussion in groups. Yes, it can work in a morning worship session if the case-study is interesting, and if it deals with issues that church members are struggling with it can be more effective educationally than a straight sermon.

Though a tad unorthodox, showing a carefully selected didactic (teaching) movie followed by an open discussion can be very effective in fostering critical thinking.

I would encourage the use of PragerU video clips for Sabbath/Sunday School class, youth fellowship or even 'big church.' They are brief, single topic issues of importance and well packaged for discussion, see https://www.youtube.com/user/PragerUniversity.

Planning, in advance, discussion/debate on topical, even controversial, issues using the research skills of youth and young adults can be a win-win situation for all.

Church leaders must have a vested interest in fostering critical thinking and this should include re-examining the lyrics of the choruses we sing in church.

I have heard of some embarrassing things sung in church. The song 'My Soul Doth Magnify the Lord' has a line "even death could not hold Him captive, even in the grave He is Lord." A clergy colleague told me that he heard a lady in church singing "even death could not hold im casket…"

Let's offer sensible worship to our Lord via critical thinking because nonsense is still nonsense even in church.

Observer 27/12/18

# DISCUSSION QUESTIONS

1. How do you think Church folk would respond to this article and why?

2. How practical or useful are the suggestions in the article and why, either way?

3. Would you suggest that your Pastor read this article, why or why not?

# Article 25

## THE CHURCH AND CULTURE

**Gist**: Provocative ideas on the topic

Several years ago I shared on this topic in a church because I find that Christians tend to have an instinctive suspicion about things dubbed 'culture', whereas non-religious folk, especially if they are social scientists, tend to convey an instinctive high regard for things dubbed 'culture.' But what is culture really?

The specialists will forgive my working definition of culture as "the time-honoured (enduring), accepted way of life of a people." Here I am thinking of a broader base of people, and the accepted way of life of such over time, than what is the lived reality of a sub-culture within a section of society.

I suggest two notions about culture for consideration. Culture is not absolute but relative, not static but dynamic. Our culture then, whoever we are, is simply what is descriptive of us, not what is prescriptive for others.

How we respond to culture may be different, but all responses deserve examination. One may respond with uncritical [or complete] acceptance of culture, based on the belief that what has been for a while as culture is from the people and thus okay.

But is this necessarily true? Even the most open-minded analyst of culture will have to admit that there are some aspects of culture that are not commendable like, say, survival by stealing (cf. praedial larceny), or corruption, very entrenched in many sections of Jamaica and defended by the Jamaicanism "ah suh de ting set." Okay? I think not.

Another response (from many Christians) is uncritical [or complete] rejection of culture. Out of ignorance, some argue that all of culture is from 'the pit of hell' and must be rejected. It amazes me how easily we speak about aspects of hell without any biblical or other grounding for our ideas. I suspect that some of us confuse what we do not like with what God could not bless in use. Unless we are privy to what the devil likes we should be careful about assigning aspects of culture to him.

As a trained and lettered musician in so-called 'classical music', I have had to offer an informed polite corrective/caution to Christians who are too glib in pronouncing on what is 'not of God' re music or other art forms. Again, my humourous point is "you cannot equate your taste with God's taste unless you think you are the 4th member of the Trinity in which case we have very serious theological problems!"

What I recommend to all re responding to culture is critical engagement of culture. This engagement is by two means: 1) informed analysis via criteria for evaluation plus progressive maturity in taste and 2) involvement while examining motive and means, all the while seeking to ascertain all the relevant facts before judging finally. I explain further.

By informed analysis via criteria for evaluation I am suggesting that we ponder the basic point that some aspects of culture are amoral (neither good nor bad in essence), other aspects may be immoral and yet others perfectly wholesome. These are basic criteria for evaluating aspects of culture.

Tunes and rhythms, in my view, are basically amoral though not impotent, but songs as such (given the lyrics) can be correctly declared as immoral or wholesome. There is no sinful C sharp or A natural and no sanctified G flat or B, hence no combination of notes forming a tune can be defensibly described in moral terms.

There is no sinful or sanctified beat, hence no combination of beats forming a rhythm can be defensibly described in moral terms. Sure, you may respond differently to one kind of rhythm as opposed to another, but the commentary is properly about your response, not about the rhythm itself. Regardless of the stimulus "my response is my responsibility!" Rhythm, because it affects your central nervous system, is powerful but is still, in my view, amoral in essence.

I recall chiding a Seminary group for applauding a visiting Jewish group after they had sung songs about Jerusalem and Israel in Chapel but the said group would have a problem if a group were to sing in chapel a Jamaican patriotic song like 'One more Jamaican gone abroad.' Maybe I just need Jesus but the fact that Jamaica is not in the Bible does not make a Jamaican patriotic song less spiritual than a song about Jerusalem.

The issue of maturity in taste has to do with the fact that as we gain more knowledge about a particular thing we can better appreciate the nature of that thing though we may still not be inclined to utilize it or love it.

# A CONTROVERSIAL CLERGYMAN

Youth and adults who claim not to like hymns in Church are often very ignorant about the nature of hymns. After even a crash course on the background and musical/lyrical nature of hymns their taste matures a bit though they may still prefer choruses. There is a trickier dimension to maturity in taste and this has to do with "...[learning] to distinguish between the subject matter and the artistry of the work, between its content and its form..." as one specialist puts it. Years ago some of my brethren including a respected clergy colleague took objection to the sculpture in Emancipation Park with one describing it as disgusting. I suspect because the lady's breasts are not within a brassiere.

Bearing in mind that the lady represents a member of our 'enslaved' ancestors (thanks Prof. Shepherd) how likely is it that she would have been wearing a brassiere? So, as I said mischievously to a friend 'if you have a pardonable partiality to breasts say you find the lady's breasts disturbing but not disgusting!'

There is great unquestioned artistry/skill behind the sculpture, admit that, even if you have a problem with its content, partial nudity.

I don't care much for classical organ music but I know and appreciate the consummate skill behind Bach's Tocatta and Fugue in D minor and the courage (nay the hubris) required to attempt to perform it.

With reference to the involvement component, self-examination especially in Church circles is key for me and one's motive for involvement can be all of self or genuinely geared toward educating/entertaining or ministering. With certain Christian audiences one needs to educate before or while utilizing the art form while in others it is best to try to inform pure and simple long before even attempting to utilize the art form.

It is never wise to pronounce against a person's use of a particular cultural element without seeking to gather as much of the available facts as possible. Give people the benefit of the doubt, you rarely if at all lose anything in the process.

Observer 4/3/19

## DISCUSSION QUESTIONS

1. What would the 'average Church leader' find most objectionable in this article?

2. What aspects of the article did you find most helpful intellectually and why?

3. Which aspects of the article would you need more clarity about from the author?

# Article 26

## COMPROMISED DEMOCRACY IN CHURCH AND STATE ELECTIONS?

**Gist**: An uncomfortable alert about how democracy is defeated

The basic notion of a democracy (from two Greek roots: *demos* [people] and *krateō* [I rule]) is rulership by a majority of the people; the basic notion of an oligarchy (from two Greek roots: *oligos* [few] and *archē* [head]) is rulership by a few.

It must not escape us then that the regular low voter turnout at elections in our history means that our democracy is being compromised or diminished somewhat. What is the calibre of a political mandate that comes from less than 50% of the electorate? Is this really a case of rulership of/by/for the people? Or have we unwittingly descended into oligarchy without being bothered by that reality?

I have been a Christian since 1967 and extremely rarely in any church that I have been a member or a Pastor has there been even a simple majority of the membership present and voting for the election of Officers or for the confirmation of a Pastor. In some churches, by established church policy/practice, a Bishop or an elected few determine who leads. I have never been a member or Pastor in any such church.

While I was on staff at a Baptist Church in Florida a putative candidate for the Senior Pastor's post got the majority of the votes and there was jubilation from those who wanted him in the post until it was pointed out that the meeting was not properly constituted for decision-making because there was not a quorum present and voting plus, the church's constitution required a two-thirds vote (not a simple majority vote) of the membership for confirmation of the Senior Pastor. They had to do it another time.

Most Pastors take it for granted that a church having voted for you wants you to continue in the post. I don't make that assumption at all. So crazy man that I am I requested, nay demanded, a vote of confidence from the circuit a few years into my 2nd pastorate in Jamaica.

## A CONTROVERSIAL CLERGYMAN

Basic democracy, it seems to me, requires that at least a half of the people being led desire the leader to continue in office. Periodic formal checks on the ground should be the norm for a leader's continuance in office, unless of course there is a term limit associated with the post.

It is an open secret that the approach that church members take re members' meetings and church elections is no higher than the general approach to national elections (general and local government).

If politically and ecclesiastically we say we prize democracy in principle, we need to examine whether our practice conforms to the principle. Oligarchy anyone?

Observer letter, 15/2/18

# DISCUSSION QUESTIONS

1. With which of the author's contentions, if any, do you most agree and why?

2. What would you say is behind the reality of low voter turnout for elections in state and church alike?

3. What's so wrong with oligarchy if the deciding few are known to be good people?

# Part V

# PUBLIC SPEAKING AND MISCELLANEOUS

# Article 27

# CHRISTOPHER HITCHENS: AN INTELLECTUAL POST-MORTEM?

**Gist**: Re a book on the relationship between atheist Hitchens and his Christian friend Larry Taunton

"[Jerry Falwell] was a petty little charlatan and toad...I think it's a pity there's not a hell for him to go to."
(Hitchens, 2007)

The book *The Faith of Christopher Hitchens: The Restless Soul of the World's Most Notorious Atheist*, 2016 by Larry Taunton is a sensitive, respectful and riveting reflection on aspects of the life of an outspoken critic of Christianity and its God by a personal friend who happens to be a self-confessed Evangelical Christian.

## PUBLIC SPEAKING AND MISCELLANEOUS

To the horror of the followers of Hitchens and the consternation of not a few evangelical Christians in the USA, Larry Taunton, founder of the Christian Organization called Fixed Point Foundation (FPF) and Christopher Hitchens were close personal friends. FPF specializes in producing recorded debates between Christians and skeptics, atheists, agnostics especially, and did several with Hitchens.

I was amazed to read that Hitchens and Taunton went on a few long road trips in the USA, before and after Hitchens' diagnosis of esophageal cancer and at Hitchens' insistence too! But get this, on one such trip after the diagnosis, both men engaged in a Bible study of John's Gospel.

The trip was from Hitchens' D.C. apartment to Taunton's home in Birmingham, Alabama, and Hitchens' wife Carol and their daughter Antonia saw them off. Taunton the driver says:

> Summer suit and Panama hat on, he kissed Carol good-bye as Antonia and I put his things in the back of my Tahoe. In addition to a small suitcase were a picnic lunch and predictably, enough Johnnie Walker [Black label] for a battalion. 'Have you a copy of Saint John with you,' he asked with a smile. 'If not you know I do actually have one.' (p.120)

## A CONTROVERSIAL CLERGYMAN

Hitchens was partial to the language of the King James Version and owned a copy. Taunton had chided him two years earlier that he had not really read the Bible, "but only cherry-picked it." (p.120)

Hitchens had his whiskey glass "nestled between his knees" and periodically drank and smoked along the way. "As I drove Christopher read aloud from the first chapter of John's Gospel. A marvelous reader with a marvelous voice, it all seemed a bit surreal...Atheist Christopher Hitchens, spectacles perched on his nose, was reading the Bible aloud in the front seat of my car." (p. 122)

I smiled when I read that on reaching John 11:25-26, mischief and mystery became married. The text reads, "Jesus said unto her, I am the resurrection, and the life: he that believeth in me, though he were dead, yet shall he live: And whosoever liveth and believeth in me shall never die. Believest thou this?"

Hitchens, according to Taunton, voices remembrance of the text and says:

> I did not recall its connection with the resurrection of Lazarus." Taunton says the text is great to which Hitchens says, 'Yes. Dickens thought so,'and then, taking his reading glasses off, he turns to me and asks: "Do you believest thou this, Larry Taunton?" His sarcasm is evident, but it lacks its customary force. 'I do.

But you already knew that I did. The question is, Do you believest thou this, Christopher Hitchens?' As if searching for a clever riposte, he hesitates and speaks with unexpected transparency: 'I'll admit that it is not without appeal to a dying man.'(p.168)

No, Taunton does not say that Hitchens proceeded to accept Jesus as his Lord and Saviour. He does say though:

There is no denying that at the time of his death, Christopher was, as now, best known for his atheism. And while this defined his public image, an intellectual postmortem indicates that it is not the key to understanding him. This was, after all, the man who admitted to me that he had never read Richard Dawkins's bestseller *The God Delusion*; who regarded Sam Harris's utilitarianism 'a weak and untenable philosophy;' and who was disgusted by Peter Singer's advocacy of infanticide...Christopher did not die the Leftist radical of his youth or the militant atheist of his adulthood. (pages 162 and 163)

I concur with atheist Michael Shermer who says of Taunton's book on the book jacket "This book should be read by every atheist and theist passionate about the truth."

Gleaner 23/7/16

## DISCUSSION QUESTIONS

1. Did the article make you want to read Taunton's book, why or why not?

2. What do you think made these two men, of such radically disparate worldviews, friends?

3. Since you may not know anything about Taunton, did you wonder if he might have bent the truth a bit to sell his book and what moved you to that position?

# Article 28

## THE YELLOW PAGES STORM IN A THIMBLE

**Gist**: A mischievous piece of advice from this irreverent clergyman

If you have a problem with the front cover of your copy of the current Jamaican Yellow Pages directory (dance hall scene) why not just flip it over to the back cover (ska/rocksteady scene), or better still, just tear off the flipping front cover.

This is a simple solution to a simple problem in my view. The cover is almost literally a flat (two-dimensional) cardboard photo, and that disturbs or turns on some of us? Give me a break.

# A CONTROVERSIAL CLERGYMAN

Now, though I am trained in music and philosophy and have been a Christian for 49 years, I would not venture to do any kind of research at a live dance hall session because I personally could not "plead the blood of Jesus" fervently enough to keep all sections of my anatomy calm. Even then my possible response to the visual stimuli in that setting would be essentially saying much more about me than about the gyrating female bodies I would be viewing.

*Apropos* this stimulus/response issue, two illustrations have been brought to my attention in recent months. One, squeeze a peeled orange as hard and as long as you can and you will never ever get lime juice from the effort.

This is because of the internal make-up of orange which determines its response to squeezing. If a skimpily clad lady or one who is not exactly small-breasted or of a small derriere turns me on sexually that response is essentially because of my internal make-up.

The other illustration relates to grains of sand in an eye as opposed to in an oyster. Sand in an eye irritates and harms but in an oyster a pearl is likely, because the make-up of the eye does not allow for a response other than irritation/harm whereas the make-up of the oyster leads to a pearl response.

## PUBLIC SPEAKING AND MISCELLANEOUS

Whether it is the sculpture at Emancipation Park, the current Yellow Pages 'dancehall cover' or whatever, let's not forget or downplay the fact that our response to any given work of art may be more suggestive of the kind of person we are than about the aesthetico-moral calibre of the work of art.

Maybe I just need Jesus, but Church leaders need to revisit their definition (if they have one) and defense of what we regard as pornography.

This Yellow Page controversy is really more like fomenting a category 5 storm in a thimble than a storm in a teacup. For the young and innocent a thimble is a tiny sewing device.

Gleaner letter 10/12/16 (modified header as above)

Observer letter 12/12/16 (as sent '...teacup storm')

## DISCUSSION QUESTIONS

1. Why would this clergyman decide to enter the fray with this article?

2. Reading 'between the lines,' what do you think he hoped to achieve or get off his chest?

3. How cogent did you find the author's point about response as opposed to stimulus?

# Article 29

## STIMULUS AND RESPONSE, REVISITED

**Gist**: Defending his provocative view on the topic

It seems that a few who read my letter to the editor about the Yellow Pages issue thought, like Mr. Robert Dalley, that I was dismissing the power of stimuli. On the contrary, I just wanted to focus on response because it is too often neglected, perhaps because it broaches the awkward notion of responsibility for whom I am and for what I do.

I am too old to be unaware of the stimulating power of a good-looking female body, even dressed normally, whether live, in a movie or in a photo. In fact, I still recall the pangs of remorse I felt when, as

# PUBLIC SPEAKING AND MISCELLANEOUS

a Christian for only a few months (in 1967), I lusted at a prostitute while on my way to a Convention at Jarrett Park in my hometown, Montego Bay.

I had no clue then as a 17-year old boy about the practical difference between admiring and lusting. Many, many years later, after I had produced material guiding folk on how to avoid lust, I saw a well-dressed lady in Spanish Town and after one look I said to myself, "A shoulda sin fi any ooman look suh good" [It should be a sin for any female to look so good]. So yes, I do know the power of stimuli.

I maintain still though that we give more serious thought to ourselves and our response, because it is no plea of mitigation to claim that women who dress to look sexy "cause you to lust". (I know that women lust at men too but just stay with my focus here). Beyond the notorious difficulty of proving causation I raise a simple point.

Since it is incontestably true that not all men would lust at the same skimpily clad or well-dressed lady, then this means that the stimulus (the lady's body seen) though powerful is not universally coercive toward sexual arousal. The variables in a given man are many, aesthetic taste, etc., but the main point remains. You do not have to be sexually stimulated by viewing anyone's body, no matter how 'good' it looks.

## A CONTROVERSIAL CLERGYMAN

If you become aroused it is because you are the kind of person that can be aroused by seeing a certain kind of female body. That is why, I raised in my letter, the grains of sand stimulus and the different response of a human eye and an oyster.

I know it is not the most comfortable thought to deal with, but it is not simplistic, Mr. Dalley, to suggest the thought that my response to any stimulus says more about me than about the stimulus.

Oh sure, society ought to be concerned about the possible negative impact certain stimuli could have on young minds and lives, even though we may not be able to argue for the probability, likelihood or certainty of the negative impact.

While executing that critical role as guides of children and youth especially, we ought also or more so to train them in self-restraint, self-mastery and character building.

Whether you are religious or not you can be trained/taught how to resist or defuse the power of certain stimuli.

Observer letter 30/12/16

PUBLIC SPEAKING AND MISCELLANEOUS

# QUESTIONS FOR DISCUSSION

1. What do you make of the author's admissions in this piece?

2. How workable is the author's suggestion in the 2nd to last paragraph?

3. Where would your sentiments be on the side of stimulus or response, and why either way?

# Article 30

## SLAVERY IN THE BIBLE MICHAEL ABRAHAMS'S READING PROBLEMS

**Gist**: A strong reminder about how to read ancient texts responsibly

The Bible is probably the only ancient text that any Mike, Mary or Marcia waxes warm about, despite stark ignorance of the book's actual texts, original languages and historical contexts (plural).

The lay critic may be very educated but (s)he and even most Christians need to understand how to read an ancient text from a different linguistic and cultural milieu than ours. I illustrate the need with the issue of slavery in the Bible, which my esteemed friend Dr. Michael Abrahams raised in his *Gleaner* column on Monday, August 28, 2014.

Most of us learned in English literature class the basic point that a text must be read in light of its context. What contextual cues do we need to bear in mind to read the Bible responsibly?

Well for starters we need to remember that slavery in the Old Testament and through the time of Jesus, though not a societal ideal, was not like the slavery we in the modern world are accustomed to reading about.

Slavery in the ancient Near Eastern world, Michael, was a universal expedient and so could not be denounced and, in an age of wars of conquest or of revenge way back then, it was the milder of two cruel options for dealing with captives: kill them or enslave them. Slavery in such an age was a species of labour relations, masters (=employers) and slaves/servants (=employees).

The Old Testament Hebrew word *'ebed* is better translated 'servant' or 'employee' rather than 'slave' because there was nothing inherently lowly or undignified in being an *'ebed*. The Ebed-Melech (literally 'servant of the King' = royal official) who rescued Jeremiah (Jer. 38:7-10) was a prestigious employee.

To be sure compensation for a 'slave' hardly rose above lodging, clothing and food but...slavery in the ancient world of the Old Testament could not practically be abolished. The best that a society could do was to regulate its operation. If we are brutally honest we would realize that not even the most progressive or libertarian thinker can even imagine a modern or future world in which some folk would not be hired by and working for other folk!

In this regard critics and even Christians miss the uniqueness of the Bible's approach to slavery. In the fundamental regulations that governed ancient Israel —the Mosaic Law—master-slave relations are humanely regulated.

Exodus 21:2-11 as societal legislation "is concerned about the rights, limits of control, and personhood of slaves..." (Walter C. Kaiser Jr., *Toward Old Testament Ethics*, 1991, 98).

Michael says of Lev. 25:44-46, "It was also permissible for [Israelites] to purchase children of foreigners, **and to treat them as property, passing them on to their own children as a permanent inheritance**." (my emphasis)

If by the bold section Michael is concluding that because the children of foreigners can be purchased and passed on to the children of Israelites, then by this tradition the children so passed on are treated as property, he is indulging a *non sequitur* based on ignorance of the linguistic and socio-cultural realities of the text in that ancient world context. It does not follow that a child passed on is regarded, let alone treated, as property!

As Philosopher/Ethicist Paul Copan advises:

> Even when the terms buy, sell, or acquire are used of servants/employees, they don't mean the person in question is 'just property.' Think of a sports player today who gets 'traded' to another team, to which he 'belongs.' Yes, teams have 'owners,' but we are hardly talking about slavery here! Rather, these are formal contractual arrangements, which is what we find in Old Testament servanthood/employee arrangements. (In his *Is God a Moral Monster?* 125)

Re Ex. 21:2-6, a slave who is given a wife by his master was not allowed to leave with her and their children during the 7th year after he became a slave because the wife (in all likelihood a slave too working off a debt) needs to liquidate the debt. Even today I think, when you have a job contract for a given period and decide to end the contract prematurely your employer is due damages from you.

## A CONTROVERSIAL CLERGYMAN

Michael blunders in his reading of Ex. 21:7-11 because of ignorance of a basic fact that ancient societies had limited collateral options (not being cash-based economies), hence one's labour power was a major basis of relational and occupational bargaining, hence debt-bondage, etc.

My friend deserves a bit of empathy though because there are linguistic difficulties surrounding the translation of the Hebrew text, but I would advise (as one familiar with the Hebrew text) that the 'selling' is not re slavery but re marriage. There is no 'sex slave' nuance here, Michael!!

Asking/expecting a fee for offering your daughter for marriage (= 'selling your daughter') was an ancient Near Eastern 'bride-price' custom and is roughly equivalent to the modern tradition of lavishing gifts upon a bride's parent(s) for the honour of marrying a desired lady.

The maximum length of service of a Hebrew slave was six years (Ex. 21:2; Deut. 15:12). When released such a slave had no financial obligations to the master and indeed the master was expressly commanded, "And when you release him, do not send him away empty-handed. Supply him liberally from your flock, your threshing floor and your winepress. Give to him as the LORD your God has blessed you." (Deut. 15:13-14, NIV). This

## PUBLIC SPEAKING AND MISCELLANEOUS

approximates our modern bonus, gratuity or a "golden handshake".

In the Mosaic code there are regulations re a master striking his slave (Ex. 21:20-21), or causing permanent injury to a slave (Ex. 21:26-27). It is simply not true that the latter text, according to Michael, "stated that it was permissible to knock out a slave's eye or teeth without punishment..." A master who by ill-temper or cruelty harms a slave was legally obligated to free the slave with exemption from any further obligation to pay back the debt with his labour power. Pardon my Ugaritic, Mike, but read the flipping text!

"...if you peruse the pages of the Bible concerning slavery, you will learn that cruelty was clearly tolerated." Like seriously, Michael? Seeing dimly through a dark glass, Friend?

Jesus Christ's radical ethic of love transformed individual lives and progressively revolutionized human relations. Paul's letter to the slave owner Philemon draws on this ethic of love and the letter was radically counter-cultural to the mores of first century AD Greco-Roman society.

Read properly with awareness of the ethics of the age, the Bible's approach to slavery is astute and subtly radical. What prohibition could not achieve at the time, progressive ethical regulation and personal transformation accomplished over time — the abolition of slavery and the ongoing improvement of industrial relations informed by Jesus' ethic of love.

We must learn to read all literature, the Bible included, accurately and responsibly.

Gleaner & Observer 3/9/17

## DISCUSSION QUESTIONS

1. How would you arbitrate this dialogue between the author and Dr. Abrahams? State your reasons after reading Dr. Abrahams' column.

2. Why shouldn't the author be disregarded as a biased defender of the Bible?

3. How would you evaluate the published summary response of one newspaper writer to the article who said, "slavery is slavery regardless?"

# Article 31

## THE PRESUMPTION OF RESOLUTIONS

**Gist**: An overlooked point about resolutions

This past Sunday (1st Sunday in January 2015) in one of the Baptist churches where I work I announced my topic as 'Learning From a Fool' (Lk.12:13-21). Of course, I readily covered myself - since they know my obsession with teaching from the pulpit - by saying that the Fool was in the text not in the pulpit.

After defending the rich Fool against preachers and Christians who fault him for selfishness and lack of neighbourliness, I went on to identify his main

## A CONTROVERSIAL CLERGYMAN

problem as a **faulty presumption** on life and on time.

Where does this arise in the text? In a string of future tenses, without any attached conditional statement, plus a presumptuous statement and command to himself.

Where is this string of future tenses? Ponder verses 18-19 from the New King James Version.

> 18. So he said, 'I will do this: I will pull down my barns and build greater, and there I will store all my crops and my goods. 19. And I will say to my soul, "Soul, you have many goods laid up for many years; take your ease; eat, drink, and be merry."'

Do you pick up the unbridled future "I will?" The whole cast of his plan, *his resolution,* is based on a presumption about the future. I say there is no conditional statement because this man—like so many of us at year's end—does not talk about his plans like how old people in the region used to talk, and possibly still do talk in some areas.

If an older person is making plans to weed the field tomorrow or go somewhere tomorrow you would usually hear the plan mixed with some conditional statement like "if life spare", "if bret inna

# PUBLIC SPEAKING AND MISCELLANEOUS

de baddy" [if breath is in the body] or "please God" or "if Jesus tarry" or "God willing."

The rich man's faulty presumption comes out in his string of future tenses without any conditional statement but it also comes out more in the statement and command he makes to himself in v. 19. The statement "Soul you have many goods laid up for many years" joined to the command "eat, drink, and be merry" is as presumptuous as it is faulty and foolish.

The man's language betrays a faulty presumption on time and life, as if he was dead sure that he would of necessity live for a long while yet.

Every New Year or other resolution is based on a presumption of extended life and time concerning which we have no guarantee, therefore our thinking and language must reflect this reality in conditional statements.

The fool's faulty presumption was checked and rebuked by God's *fatal pronouncement* in v. 20:

"Fool, **this night**, your soul **is required** of you, then who will get what you have piled up?" (Chisholm's rendition)

The language of God here is very vivid and instructive. Contrary to the man's plans for many years, the fatal pronouncement came on the same day he spoke, reflected in the Greek present tense 'is

## A CONTROVERSIAL CLERGYMAN

required' (though most translations have 'will be required'). The expression 'is required', meaning, 'is demanded back,' is the language of a banker who, having lent, is now foreclosing on the loan.

We may talk as eloquently as we might about the 'right to life' in our little human legal enterprises, but let us never forget that at the most fundamental level, life is a loan from God and God can foreclose that loan of your life when He sovereignly pleases.

All I ask is that we reckon with the presumption beneath all of the resolutions we made for 2015, and if we have not yet done so revisit them and add a conditional statement "if God…"

Observer 12/1/15, Gleaner 18/1/15

## DISCUSSION QUESTIONS

1. What is behind your initial response to the article?

2. Which aspects of the author's reasoning did you find the weakest?

3. Comment critically on the author's argumentation.

# Article 32

## FOR PUBLIC SPEAKERS AND SINGERS

**Gist**: pointers on the topic

For many years now I have been troubled by the pronunciation howlers I hear from people who ought to know better. Such persons include Prime Ministers and other Parliamentarians, Parsons, Lawyers, Doctors, Lecturers/Teachers, radio and TV personnel and Company Executives.

Mastering standard English pronunciation is not easy but possible, and in this piece I wish to provide a few basic guidelines and suggestions.

# A CONTROVERSIAL CLERGYMAN

The basic rules are the same for singers as well as public speakers and even writers.

For singers and speakers though, the sound of the word takes priority over the look or spelling of the word. We have to contend not only with silent letters in English but also with the overlooked fact that the name of some consonants begins with a vowel sound, e.g. L, M, N, R, S and X.

The 'e' or 'a' vowel sound precedes all of these and so technically they begin as vowels not as consonants. (That is why you would say (and write too), "She has an M.A. in modern languages" not "She has a M.A...") The old rule 'a' or 'thuh' before a consonant and 'an' or 'the' before a vowel means a vowel sound.

Know too that some vowels that begin words begin with the sound of a consonant. Union, Universe and Unity are pronounced with an initial 'y', therefore, they begin with a consonant. So, we get in sound "Thuh unity needed in this party..." rather than "The unity needed in this party..."

Don't freak out now when I inform that 'Y' is a consonant at the beginning of a word but a vowel elsewhere!

The final 'e' in 'where, there and are' is silent; therefore, these words end in consonants for the singer.

# PUBLIC SPEAKING AND MISCELLANEOUS

The 'h' in 'hour, honour and heir' is silent; therefore, these words begin with a vowel sound. Even very educated Jamaicans struggle with the aspirate at times.

The 'w' in 'write and wrong' is silent, therefore they begin with the special and tricky consonant 'r.'

'One' and 'once' are pronounced as 'won' and 'wonce'; therefore, they begin with a consonant sound.

The consonant 'r' is tricky for singers especially because it tends to impede the 'open throat' approach to singing with ease. The basic rule of thumb for sounding this consonant is easy to get. Never 'r' before a consonant or pause (punctuation or dramatic), always 'r' before a vowel.

So, to illustrate with a word that Christians (and others) love to use but end up abusing so often, 'Lord'. Following the rule concerning 'r,' this word is always said or sung as if it was spelt Lawd, not the Jamaican Laad though.

As I said at a very recent seminar for singers, applying the rule re 'r' makes you sound a bit 'stoosh' (as we say in Jamaica), but apply it nonetheless. So, to illustrate further I give you the phonetic spelling of how a very apt line from a popular hymnic prayer would be when the unnecessary 'r's are omitted: 'Deah Lawd and Fathur of mankind, fohgive ow

# A CONTROVERSIAL CLERGYMAN

foolish ways.' The 'er' ending of words like mother, father are rendered as 'uh', so mothuh, fathuh with the 'r' added if the next word begins with a vowel.

You may have been pronouncing/singing as you should all along but now you have an idea why you were doing what you have been doing.

Now to a few suggestions/corrections for public speakers. The now seemingly popular pronunciation of 'refer' and prefer' as if the 'ref' syllable is like that in referee is wrong! Treat this syllable as if it was 'rif' and the accent goes to the following syllable.

Data and media are plural words media folk! Proximity is always near, so 'close proximity' indulges a redundancy. Ever heard of distant proximity?

Help is available for the confessedly needy!

Observer, 1/6/17

## DISCUSSION QUESTIONS

1. What if anything did you discover that you did not know before?
2. Where in our system of education would/should one learn these pointers?
3. Should folk be concerned about these pointers since they are being understood in communic-ation without them?

# Article 33

## PUBLIC SPEAKING: PROBLEMS AND SOLUTIONS

**Gist**: Pointers for this dreaded necessity

Media houses and denominations are to blame for the gaffes (grammatical and especially pronunciation) their employees make because they do not provide the badly needed basic training in speech conventions and mastering pronunciation for them. Preachers and electronic media personnel especially but executives generally who must speak in public need and deserve this training and it is available. Contact the Caribbean Graduate School of Theology (755-4645).

# A CONTROVERSIAL CLERGYMAN

I have heard too many hosts (and guests) on radio/TV treating words like media, data, criteria and phenomena as if they are singular in number when they are all plural words and have different singular forms like medium, datum, criterion and phenomenon.

In a TV commercial I hear the now popular mangling of respiratory as respitory and veterinary as vetnary. Though it may sound crazy, more words than you would assume beginning with an 'e' are pronounced as if they begin with an 'I.' A few examples are English, engineer, enfranchise, exhaustion, electricity and electorate.

When to use 'less' as opposed to 'few' seems to be a problem for many. So, concerning the number of security personnel in certain areas we hear, "there were less soldiers and police seen..." The basic rule is, if you can count the entity in question use few[er]; if the entity is uncountable use less, so "there were fewer soldiers and police seen."

"There is less water in the dam now, or there are fewer gallons of water in the dam now."

Farther vs. further is also problematic for some. I tell my students to use farther for **physical** distance and further for **conceptual** distance. For example, "Ms. Green, let's take your argument a bit further and see where it leads" or "I refuse to go one foot

# PUBLIC SPEAKING AND MISCELLANEOUS

farther on this hike; I am dead beat and very hungry."

Close proximity, I say again, (mademoiselle B.G.) involves a redundancy because proximity is close. Ever heard of distant proximity? Church folk who lead worship need to avoid the redundant entreaty/command, 'stand to your feet' as opposed to what, doing a hand stand? The simple 'please stand' is good enough.

Now for a few tips that may not be known by many.

The expression for a repeated event is 'time and again,' **not** 'time and time again'; 'when the boot is on the other foot' is the original for the now popular, 'when the shoe is on the other foot,' meaning when the tables are turned; it is really Pandora's jar not box!

Technically, Rev. (short for reverend) must be followed by first **and** last name, not just by surname; otherwise you say, the Rev. Mr./Mrs./Ms. followed by surname only. This can be quite cumbersome in speech and in writing, so you may get around this by calling the person Brother or Sister or Pastor (if the clergy person is a Pastor, but bear in mind that not all clergy persons are pastors). I am no longer a pastor but still a Reverend.

## A CONTROVERSIAL CLERGYMAN

The British convention for a clergyperson with an earned doctorate (as opposed to an honourary one) is Dr. the Rev., whereas the American styling is Rev. Dr.

As I said earlier, training in these matters is available through the CGST.

Observer 18/6/18

## DISCUSSION QUESTIONS

1. Who among the mentioned target groups really cares about these pointers?

2. What explains the seeming ignorance about these pointers, not having been taught or forgetfulness through lack of use?

3. Some language conventions change with time but how does one know for sure when a settled change has happened?

# CONCLUSION

You have been kind enough to subject your mind to my mischievous thoughts, intellectually, and for that I am deeply grateful.

I may have caused you to rethink or think more deeply on some issues, to smile or laugh with me on others and though not necessary you may even reluctantly have agreed with some of my controversial ideas.

Exercising the mind by doing mental battle with **all** ideas has been my encouragement to students and congregations alike.

If, after wading through even sections of the book, you have been stimulated to be more critical in your reading and thinking habits then my living/writing has not been in vain.

Be gracious enough to encourage others to probe my ideas on your favourite section(s) of the book and maybe even foster dialogue on same in your circle.

Above all else just continue to use well your God-given brain wherever you may be.

# ACKNOWLEDGEMENTS

Many persons have affected my life and ministry over the years, too many to name here, but special note must be made of a few dear friends in Barbados who have been sacrificing for my ministry over many years and have made this book possible. For financial help to publish, SL and PW and for proof-reading help, one-time missionary to Jamaica, Ms. Marion Manning.

For technical formatting, Ms. Morticqua Murray of the Caribbean Graduate School of Theology and my one and only Beloved 'Big Daughter' Antoinette.

May your reward come to you before the Rapture and beyond.

The articles were first printed, mostly in the Jamaica Observer, but also in the Jamaica Gleaner on the dates at the end of each article.

# REFERENCES

Antonio, Gene. 1987. *The AIDS Cover-up? The Real and Alarming Facts About AIDS.* Ignatius Press.

Beckwith, Francis and Gregory Koukl. 1998. *Relativism: Feet Firmly Planted in Mid-Air.* Michigan: Baker Books

Beckwith, Francis J. 1993. *Politically Correct Death: Answering Arguments for Abortion Rights.* Grand Rapids Michigan: Baker Books

Boswell, John. 1980. *Christianity, Social Tolerance, and Homosexuality.* Chicago: Chicago Press

Camus, Albert. 1956. *The Rebel.* Penguin Books

Cicero. 1852. *De Legibus.* Roman Republic

Copan, Paul. 2011. *Is God a Moral Monster?* Michigan: Baker Books

Fridhanler, Louis. 1968. *Biology of Gestation* (vol. 1). New York: Academic Press

## PUBLIC SPEAKING AND MISCELLANEOUS

Gagnon, Robert. 2002. *The Bible & Homosexual Practice*. Nashville, Tennessee: Abingdon Press

Guinness, Os. 2000. *When No One Sees: The Importance of Character in an Age of Image*. NavPress Pub Group.

Kaiser, Walter C. Jr. 1991. *Toward Old Testament Ethics*. Grand Rapids: Zondervan

Leff, Arthur. 1979. "Unspeakable Ethics, Unnatural Law"

Guillebaud, Harold E. 1949. *Some Moral Difficulties of the Bible*. Intervarsity Press

Montgomery, John W. 2012. *Christ as Centre and Circumference: Essays Theological, Cultural and Polemic*. Eugene, Oregon: Wipf & Stock Publishers.

_____. 1981. *Slaughter of the Innocents*. Westchester, Illinois: Crossway Books

_____. 2019. *Human Rights & Human Dignity*. Grand Rapids: Zondervan

Moore, Keith L. 1977. *The Developing Human: Clinically Oriented Embryology*. Philadelphia: Saunders Publishing

Moreland, J.P. and William Craig. 2003. *Philosophical Foundations for a Christian Worldview*. Downers Grove, Illinois: Intervarsity Press

Nathanson, Bernard. 1983. *The Abortion Papers: Inside the Abortion Mentality*. Frederick Fell Pub

Nietzsche, Friedrich. 2010. *The Antichrist*. Soho Books [originally published 1885]

Noebel, David. 2006. *Understanding the Times*. Summit Press

Patten, Bradley. 1968. *Human Embryology* (3rd edition). Blakiston Division, McGraw-Hill

Pojman, Louis. 2010. *Ethical Theory: Classic and Contemporary Readings*. Boston: Cengage Learning

Patten, E.L. et. al. 1975. *Pathology of the Fetus and the Infant*. Chicago: Book Medical Publishers.

Taunton, Larry. 2016. *The Faith of Christopher Hitchens: The Restless Soul of the World's Most Notorious Atheist*. Nashville, Tennessee: Nelson Books

## PUBLIC SPEAKING AND MISCELLANEOUS

Thompson, Judith Jarvis. 1986. Essay: *'Unplugging the Violinist.'*

Willard Dallas. 2012. *Renovation of the Heart.* Colorado Springs: The Navigators Press

# ABOUT THE AUTHOR

Clinton Albert Chisholm has been married for 43 years to Flora and they have two adult children, Antoinette (Lashley) and Samuel and a grandson, Cameron. Flora is a tenured Professor of Biology at Valencia College in Kissimmee, Florida.

He worked in the Resident Magistrate's Courts in Montego Bay from 1968 (straight out of high school) and resigned in 1974 as Actg. Deputy Clerk of Courts to study at the Jamaica Theological Seminary (B.Th. honours); via Jamaica School of Music (A.T.C.L and L.R.S.M. in solo singing performance [to train singers not to sing solos he says, a little known fact is that he entered the classical music singing division in the Jamaica Cultural Development Competition and won the National Award for Best Soloist in

1979]); University of the West Indies/UTCWI (B.A. theology, upper 2nd honours); Sheffield University, England (M.A. biblical languages); Biola University, USA (M.A. Christian apologetics, with highest honours); The International Academy of Apologetics, Evangelism and Human Rights, France (F.C.A., Fellow in Christian Apologetics, Founder/Director of the Academy, Prof. John Warwick Montgomery said of Chisholm "in the written exam for the fellowship he got one of the highest marks and gave the best oral [Fellow's] defence in the history of the Academy").

Chisholm is regarded as the leading and most qualified Christian Apologist in the Caribbean and was awarded the honourary D.D. by the Caribbean Graduate School of Theology in 2005 for his work in Apologetics.

This is his 4th publication. The earlier ones being *A Matter of Principle* (1997, 2004), *Revelations on Ras Tafari*, (2008, 2014) and *Youth Discipleship* (2016). He was consulting editor for the pioneering 1998 work *Chanting Down Babylon: The Rastafari Reader and* has produced 24 Christian Education CDs. He served as a twice-weekly columnist for the now defunct *Jamaica Record*.

He resides in St. Cloud, Florida with his wife, Flora.

# A CONTROVERSIAL CLERGYMAN

**NOTE:** For feedback, consultation or speaking engagements contact Rev. Chisholm at cchisholm81@gmail.com. Kindly submit a review on Amazon or the platform where you bought this book. Thank you.

www.ingramcontent.com/pod-product-compliance
Lightning Source LLC
Chambersburg PA
CBHW022006100426
42738CB00041B/357